Story
of one
Cedar

Marina Chernova

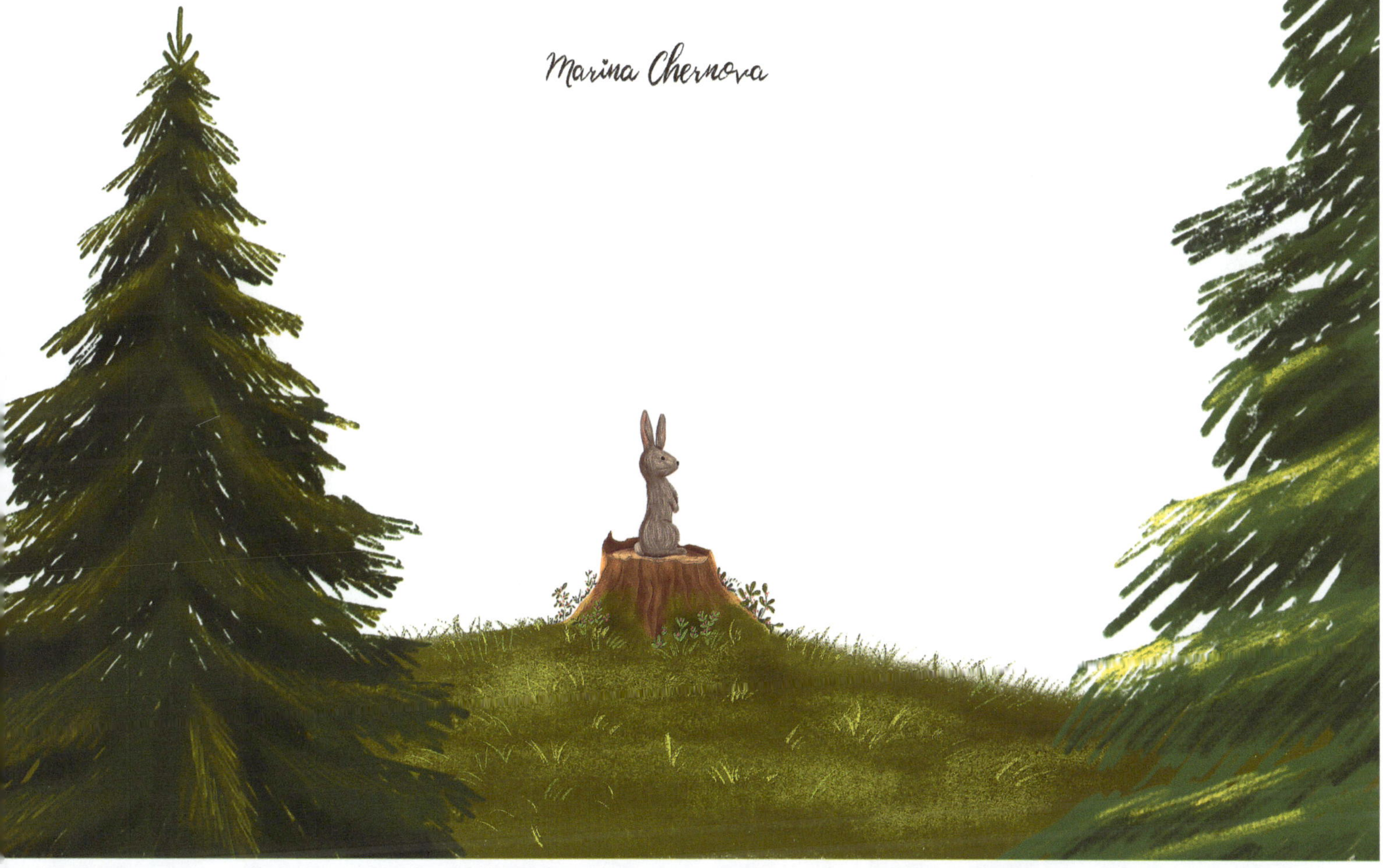

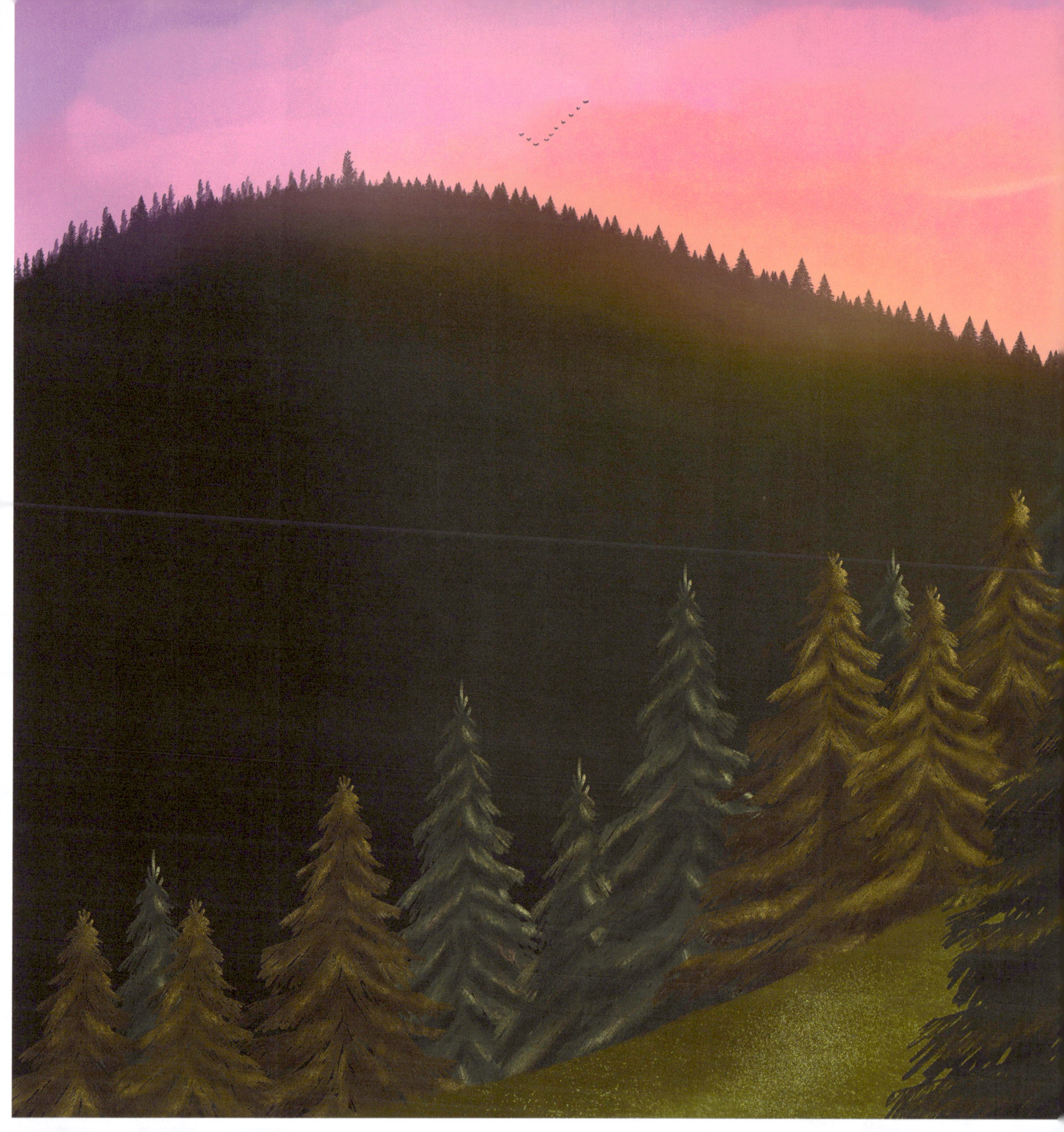

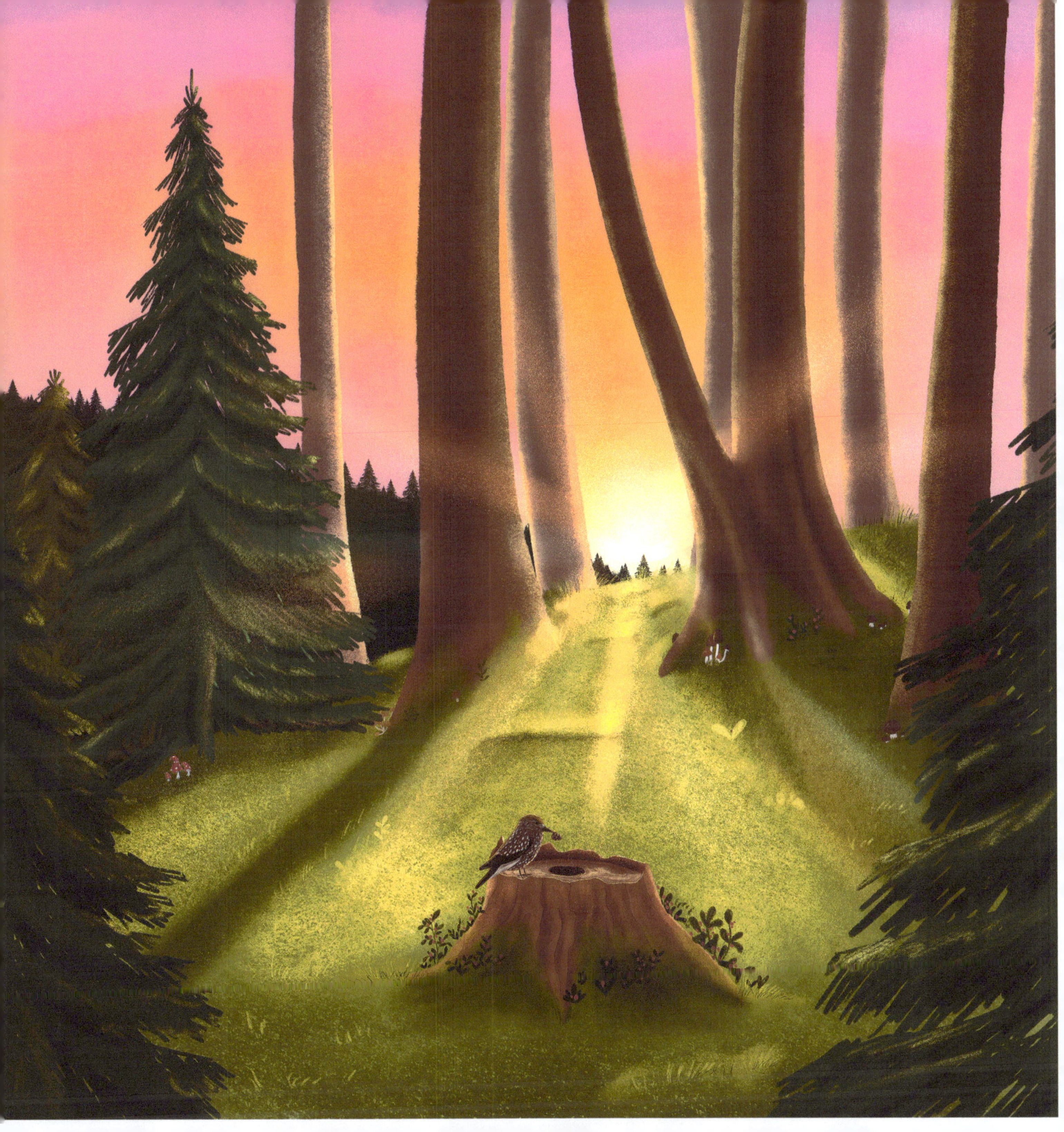

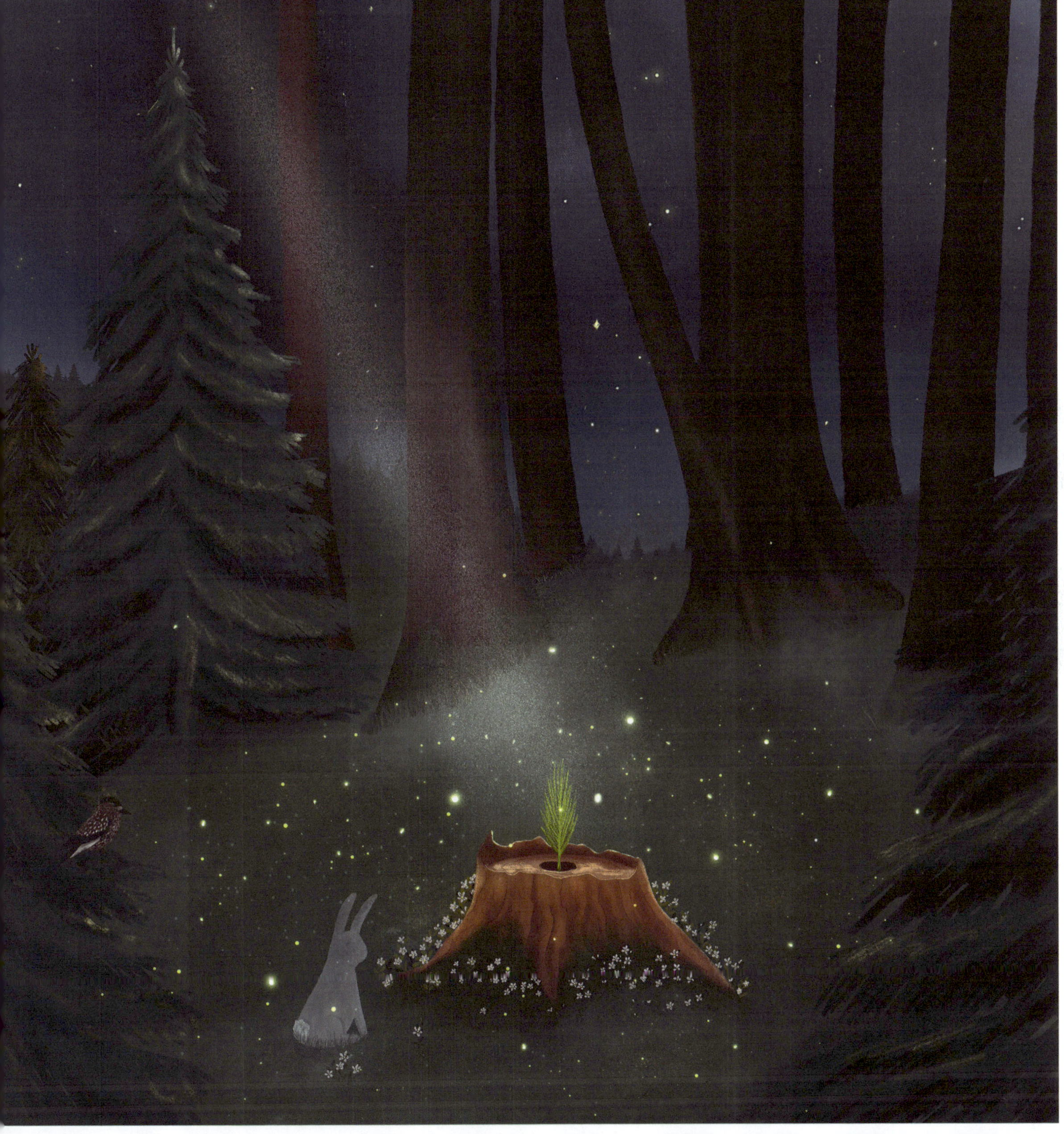

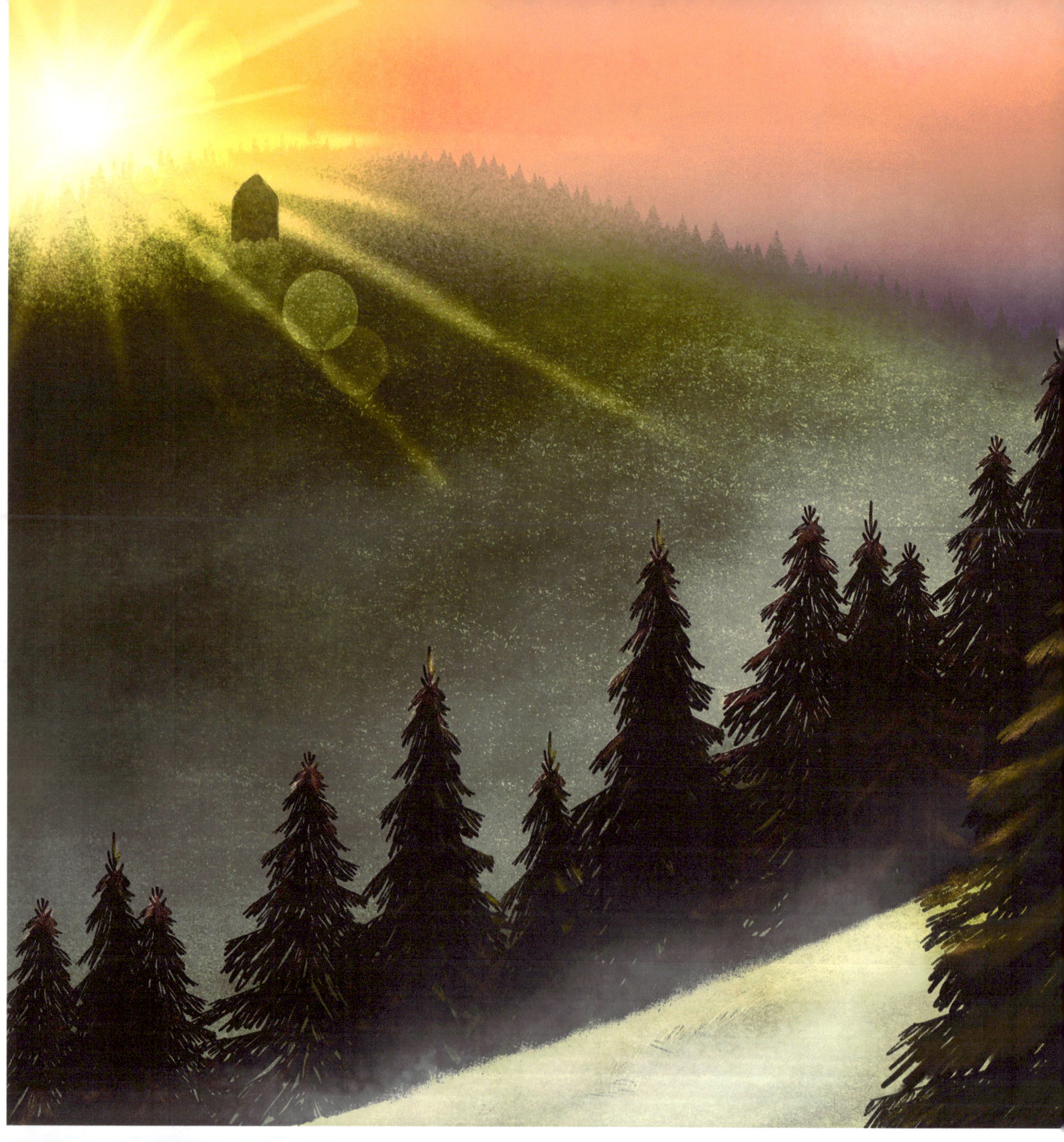

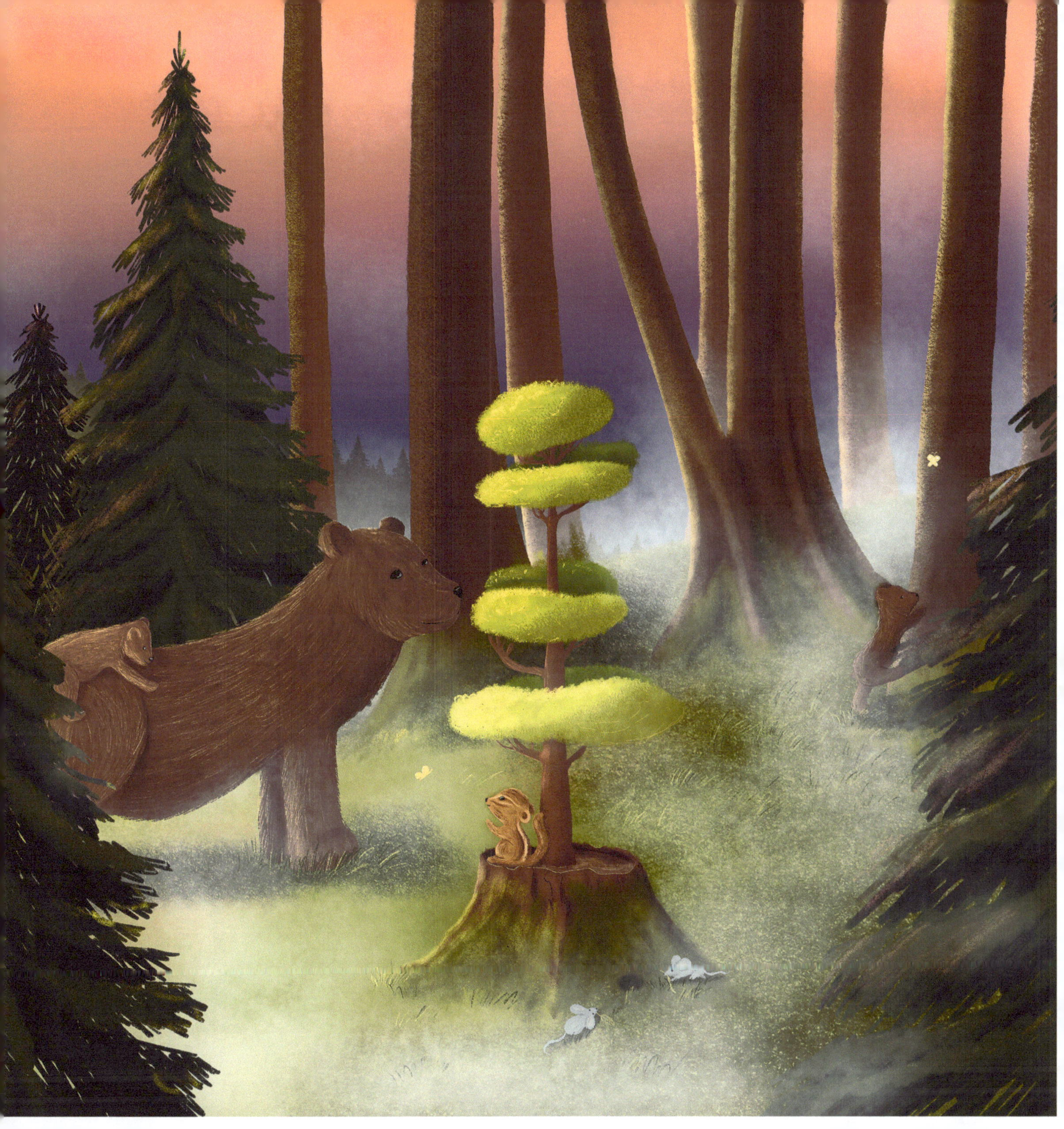

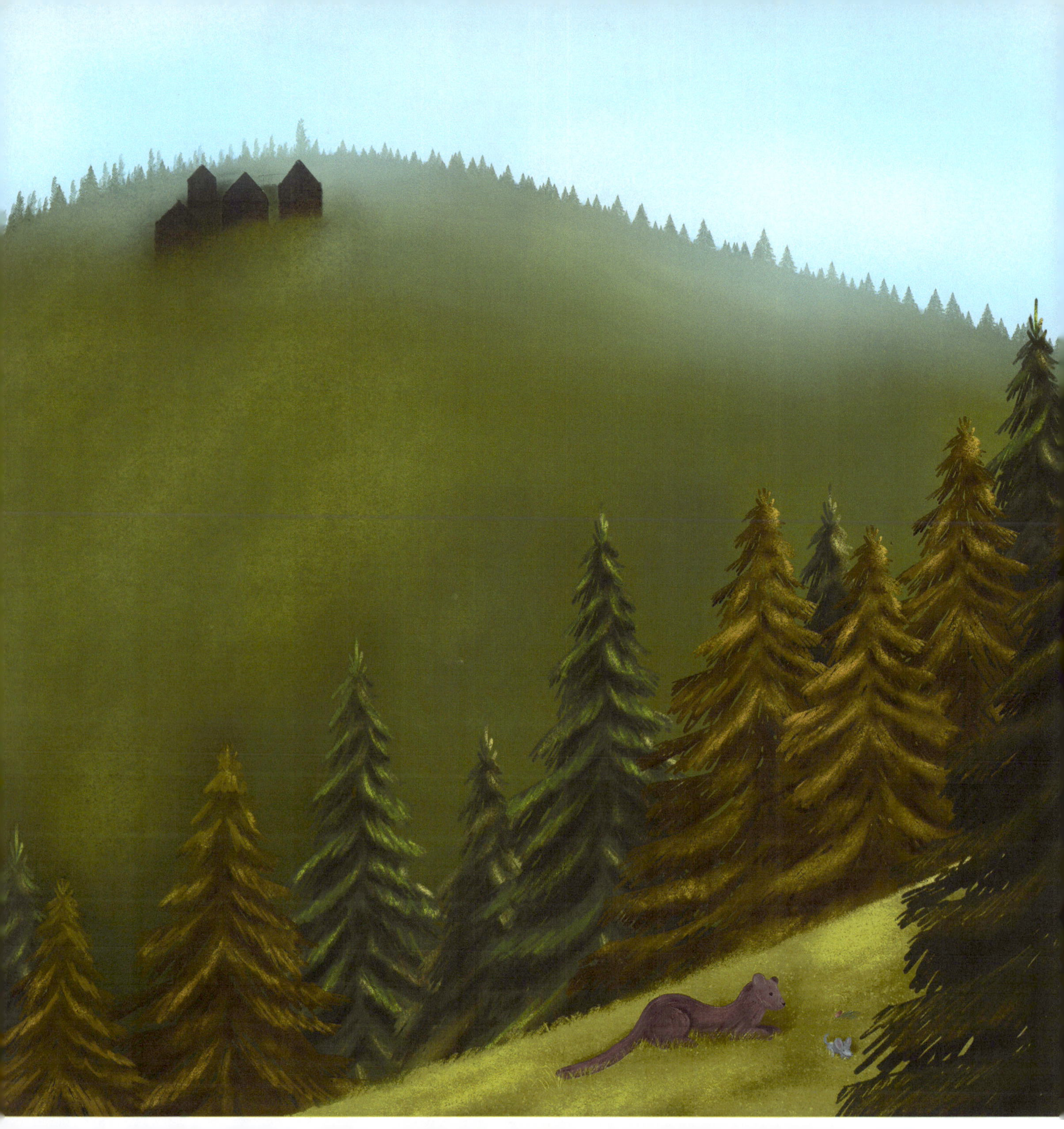

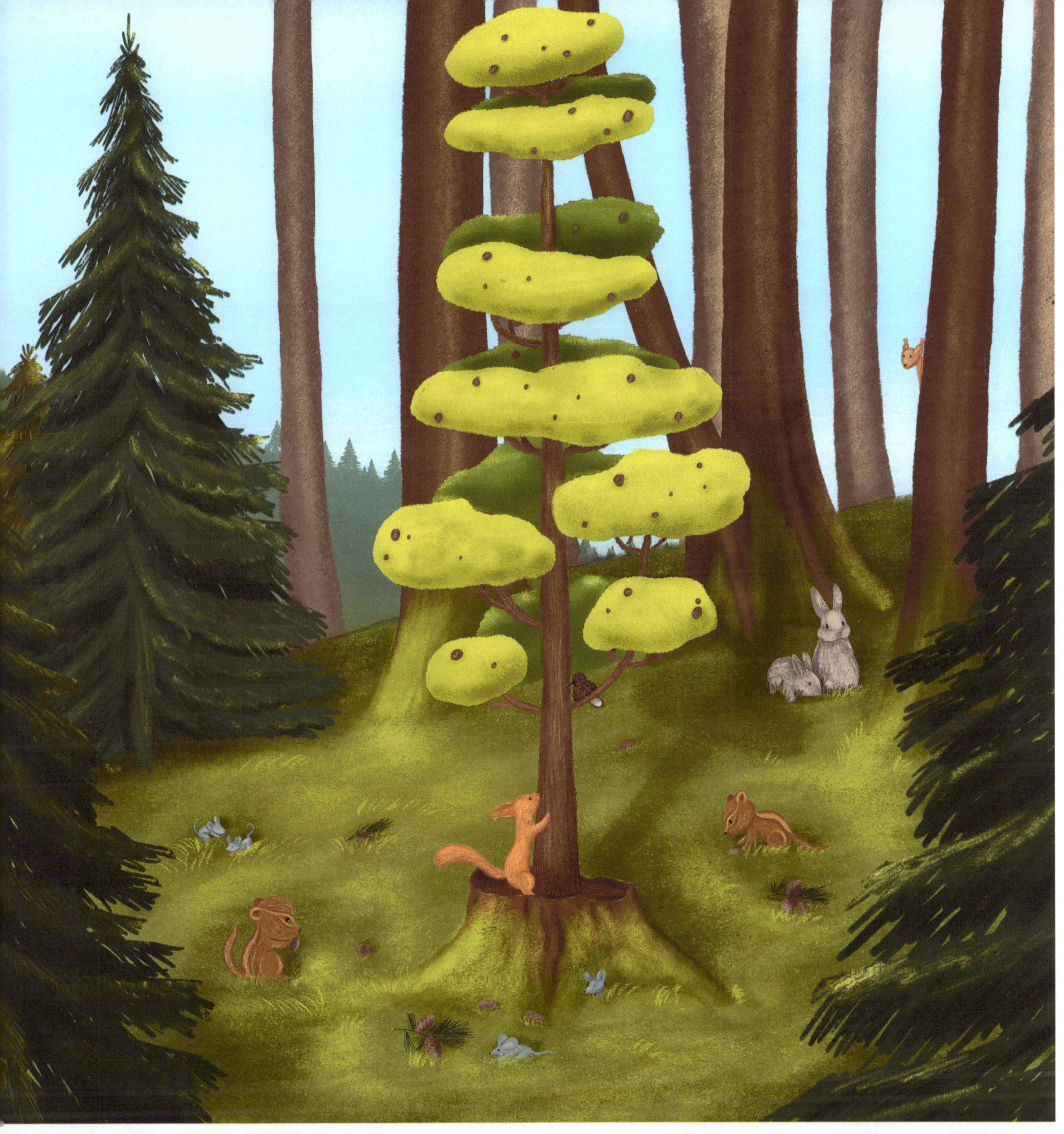

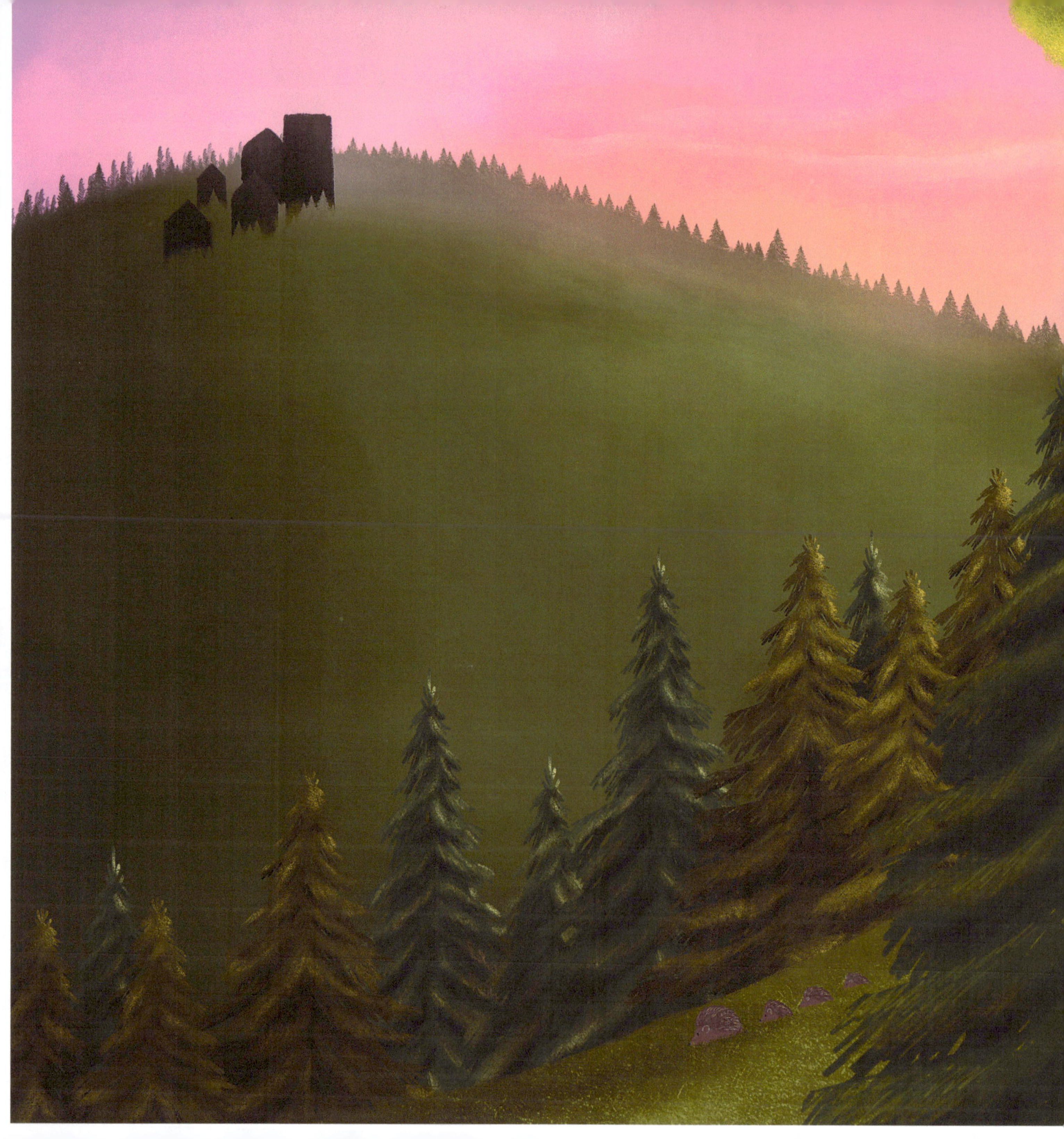

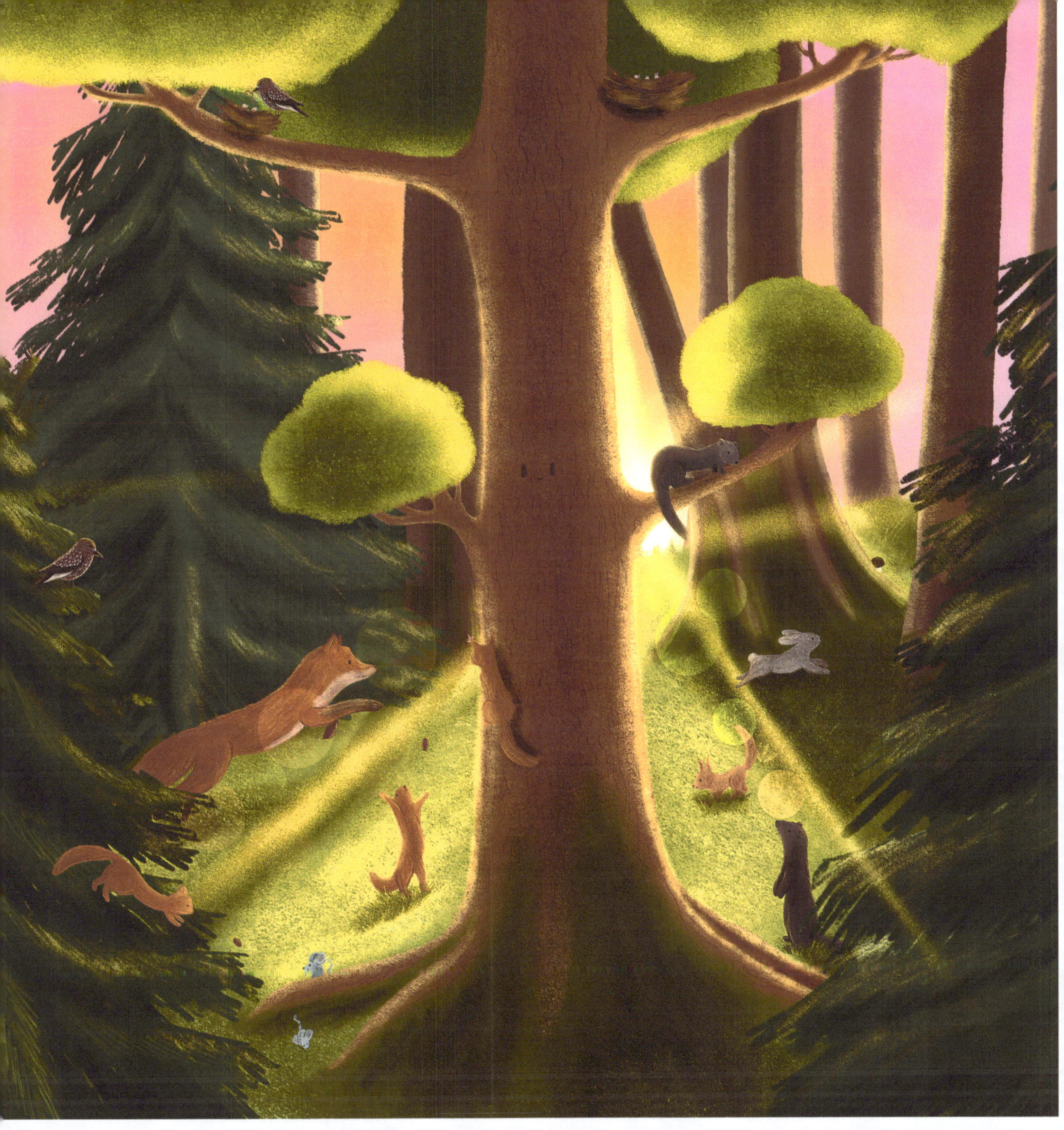

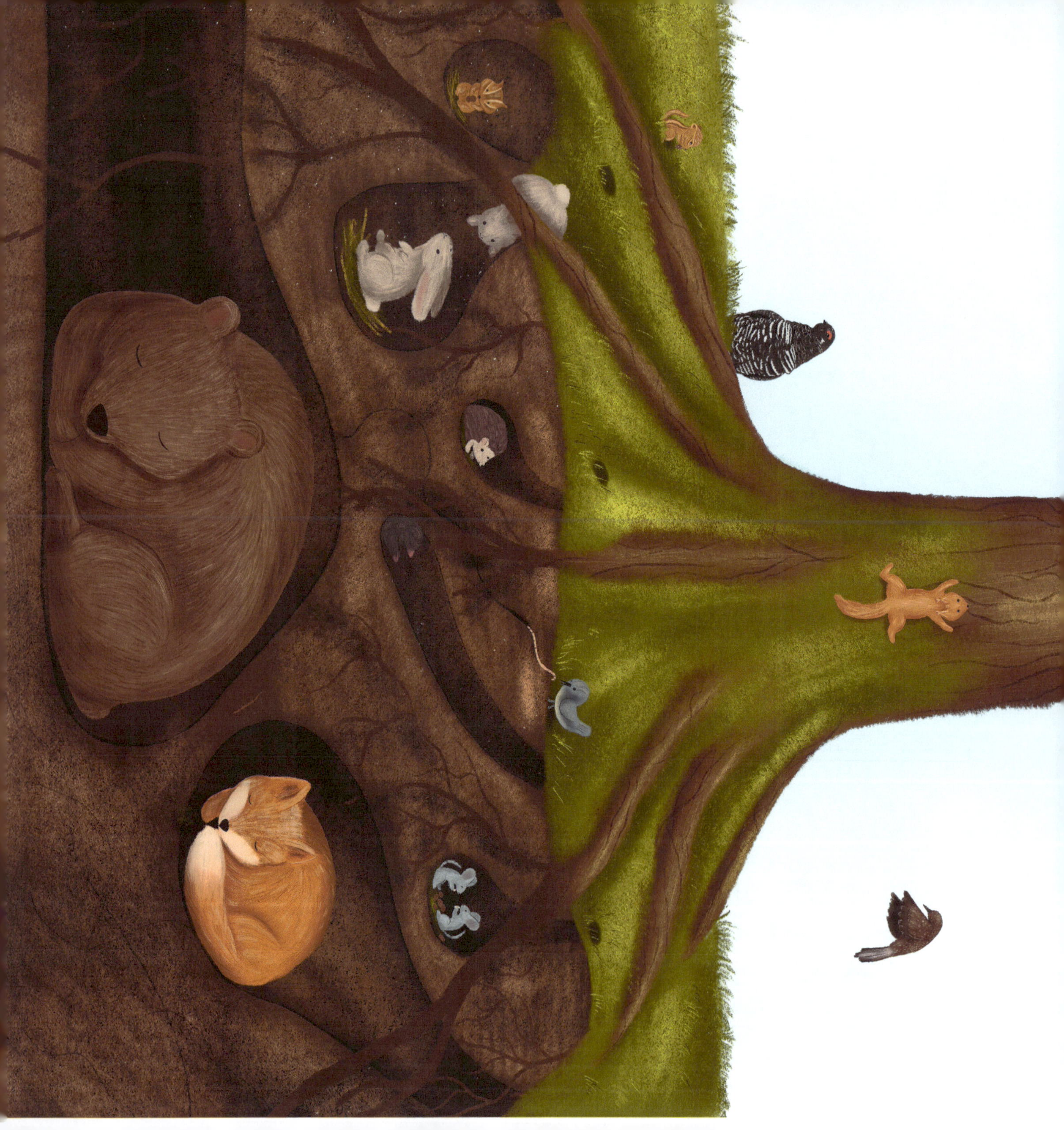

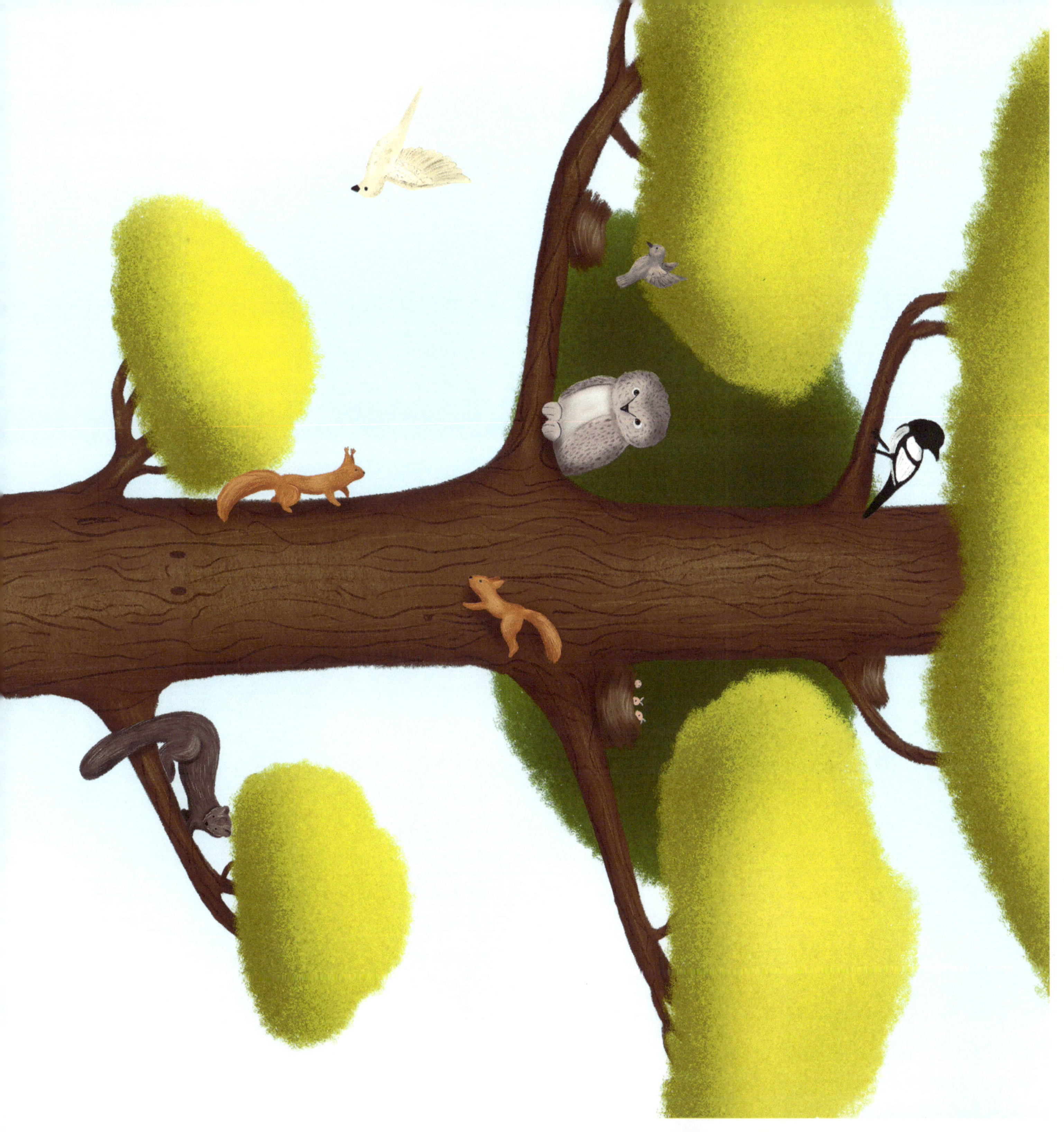

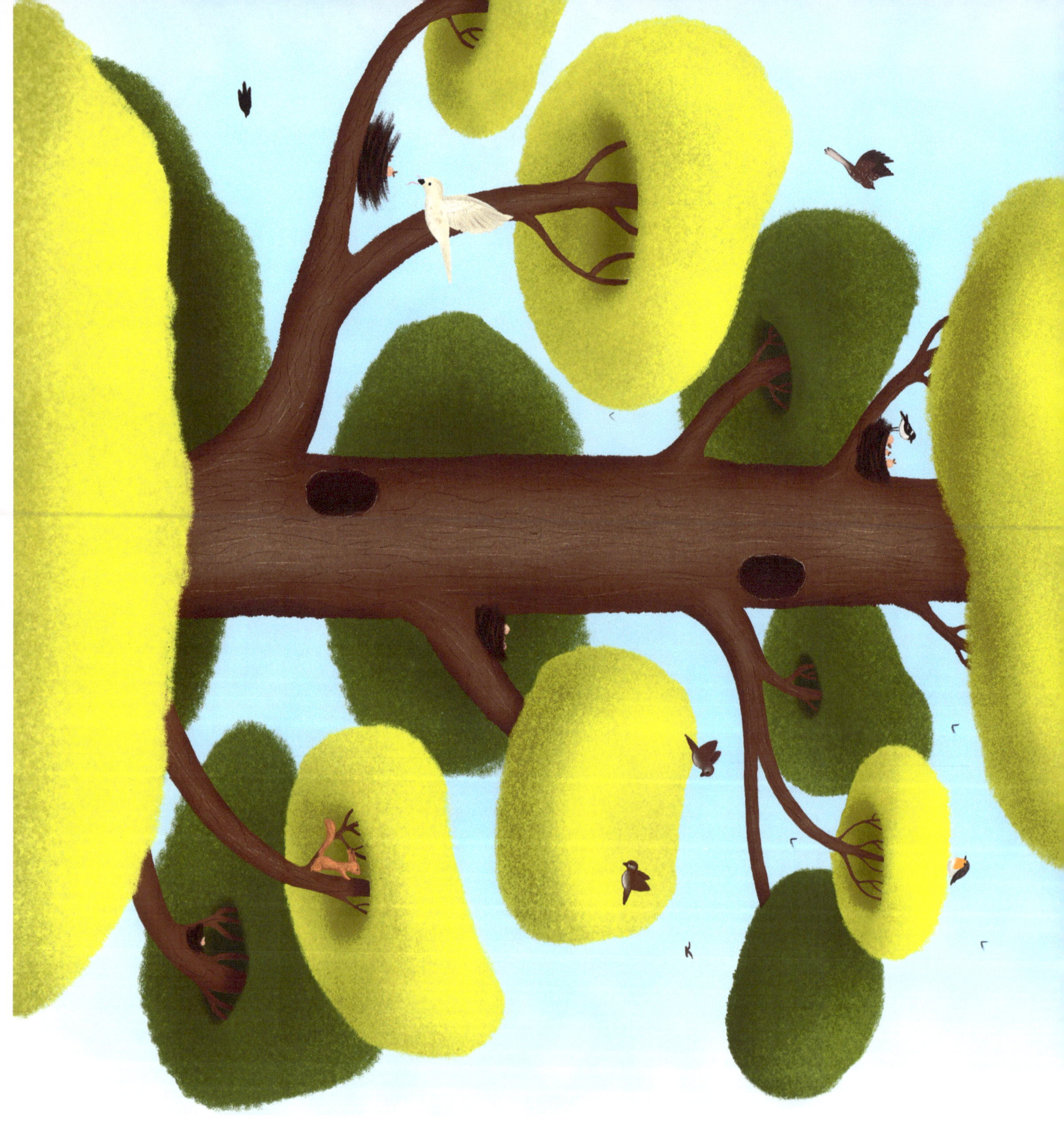

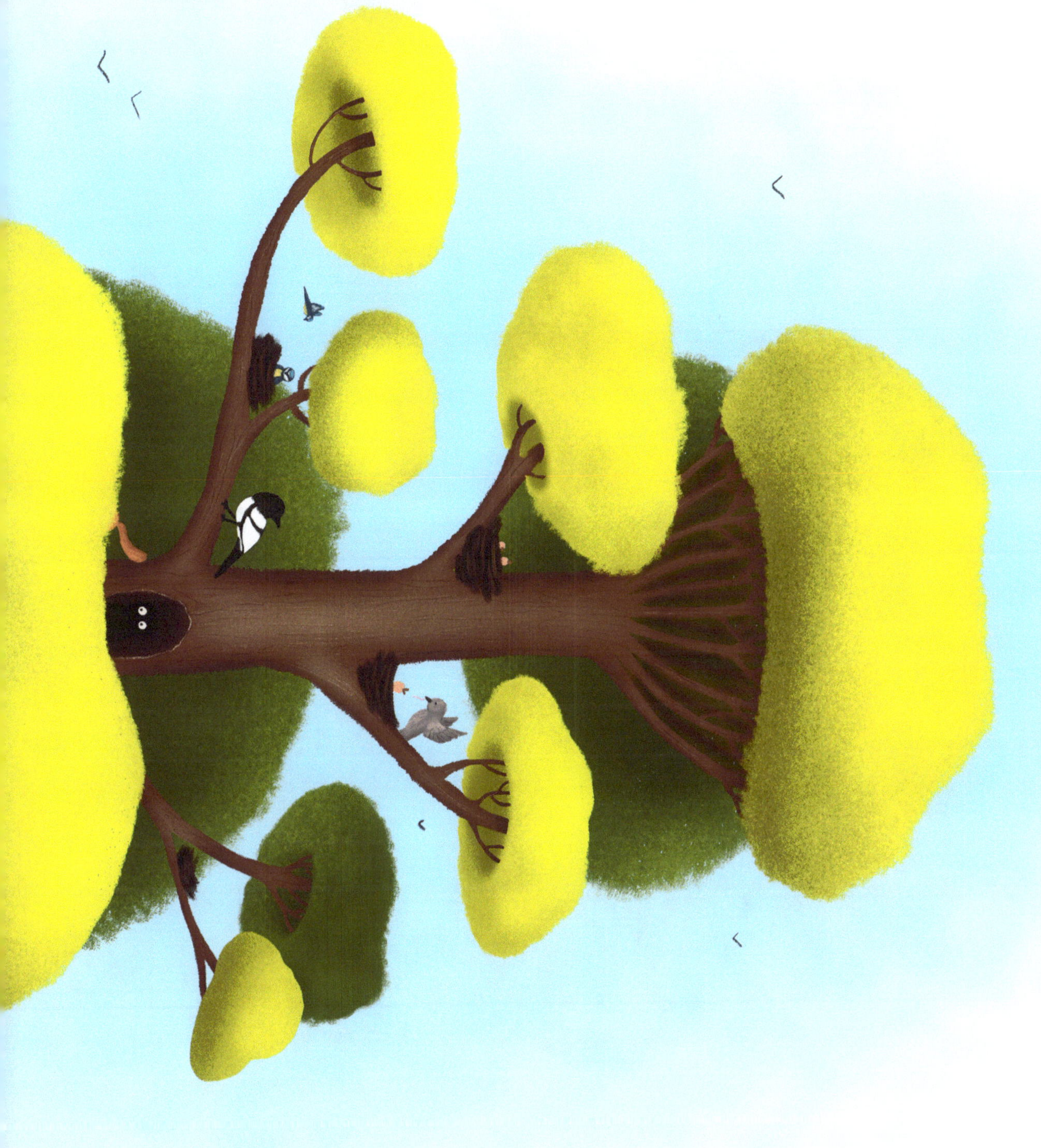

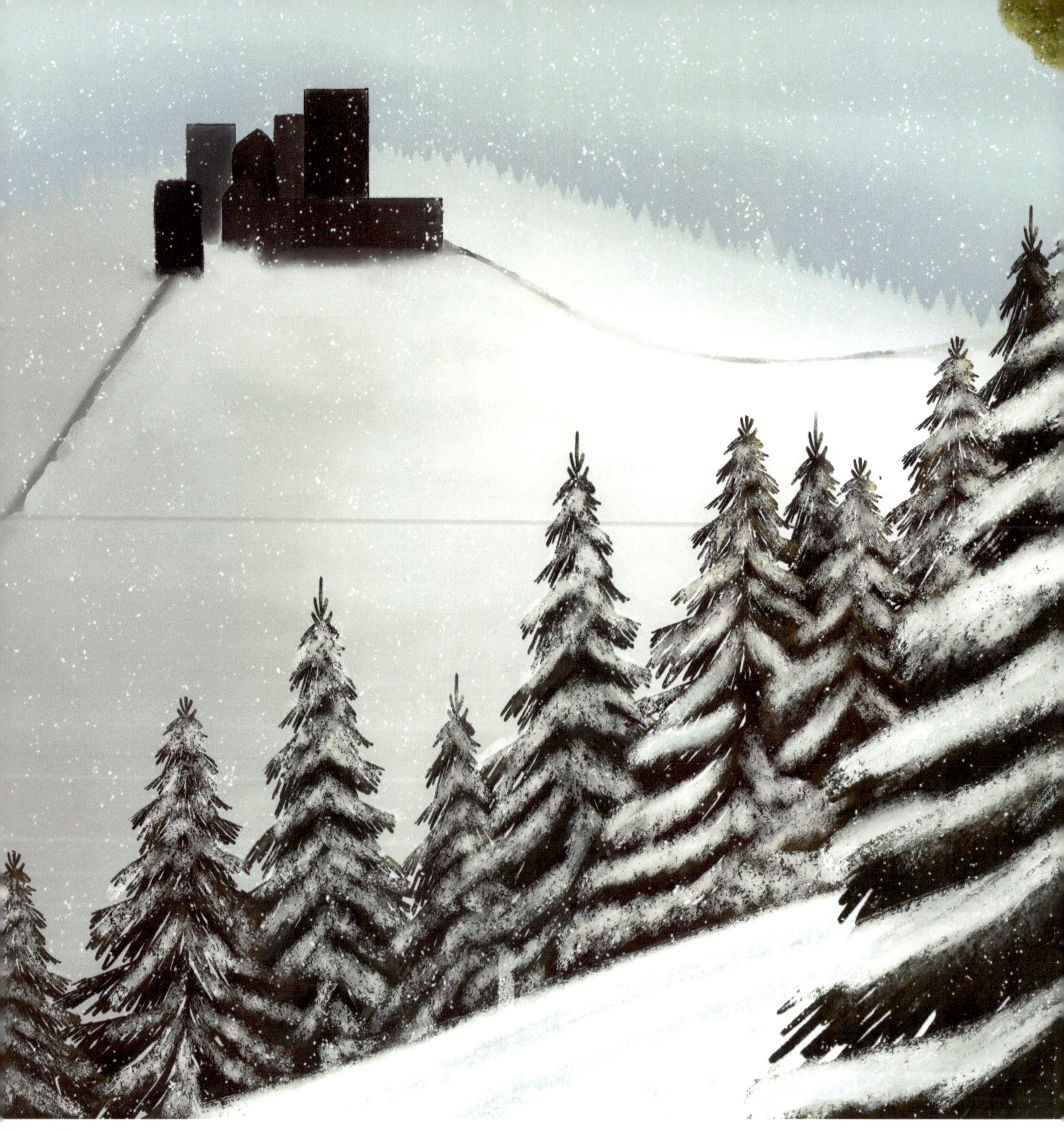

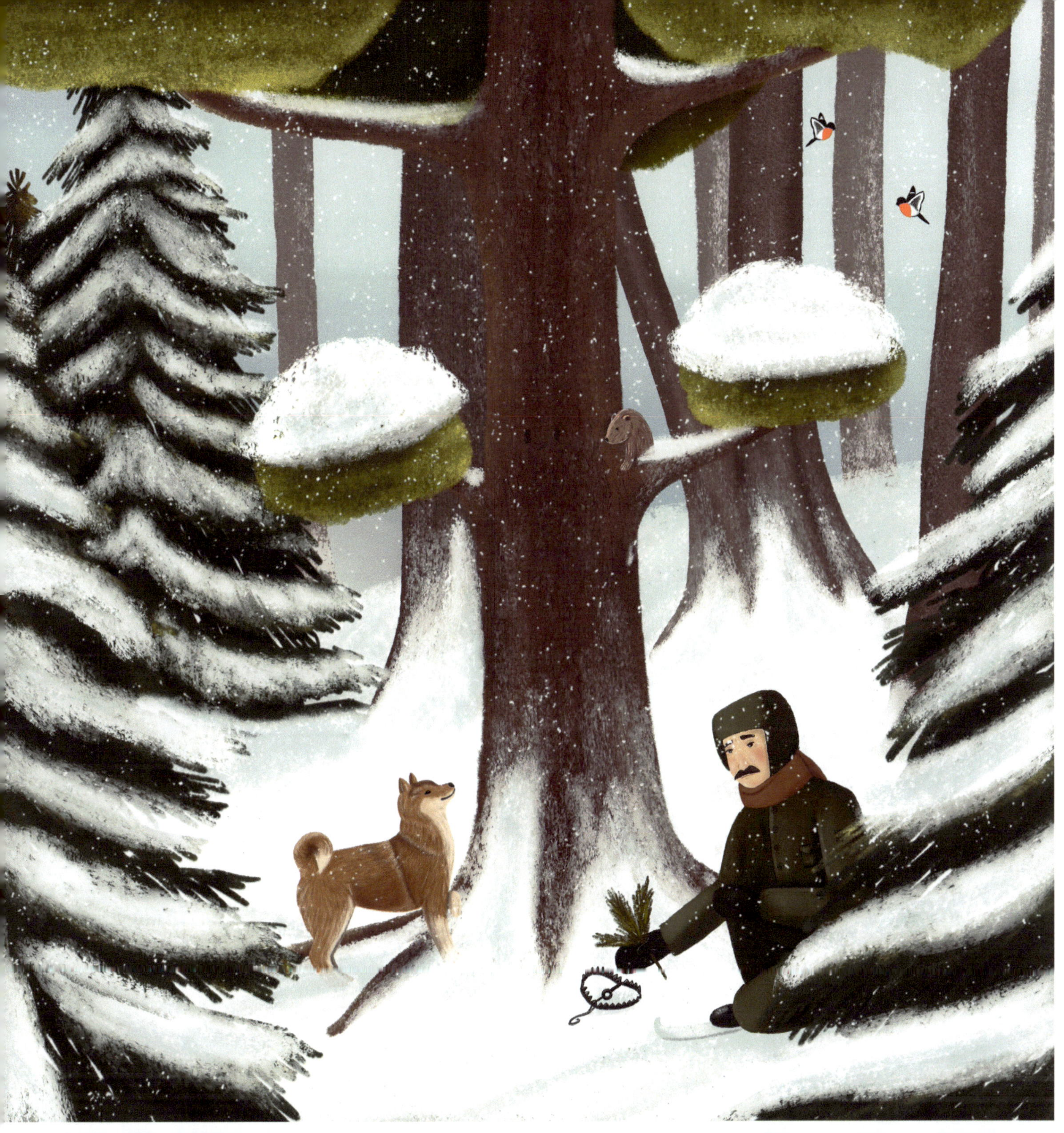

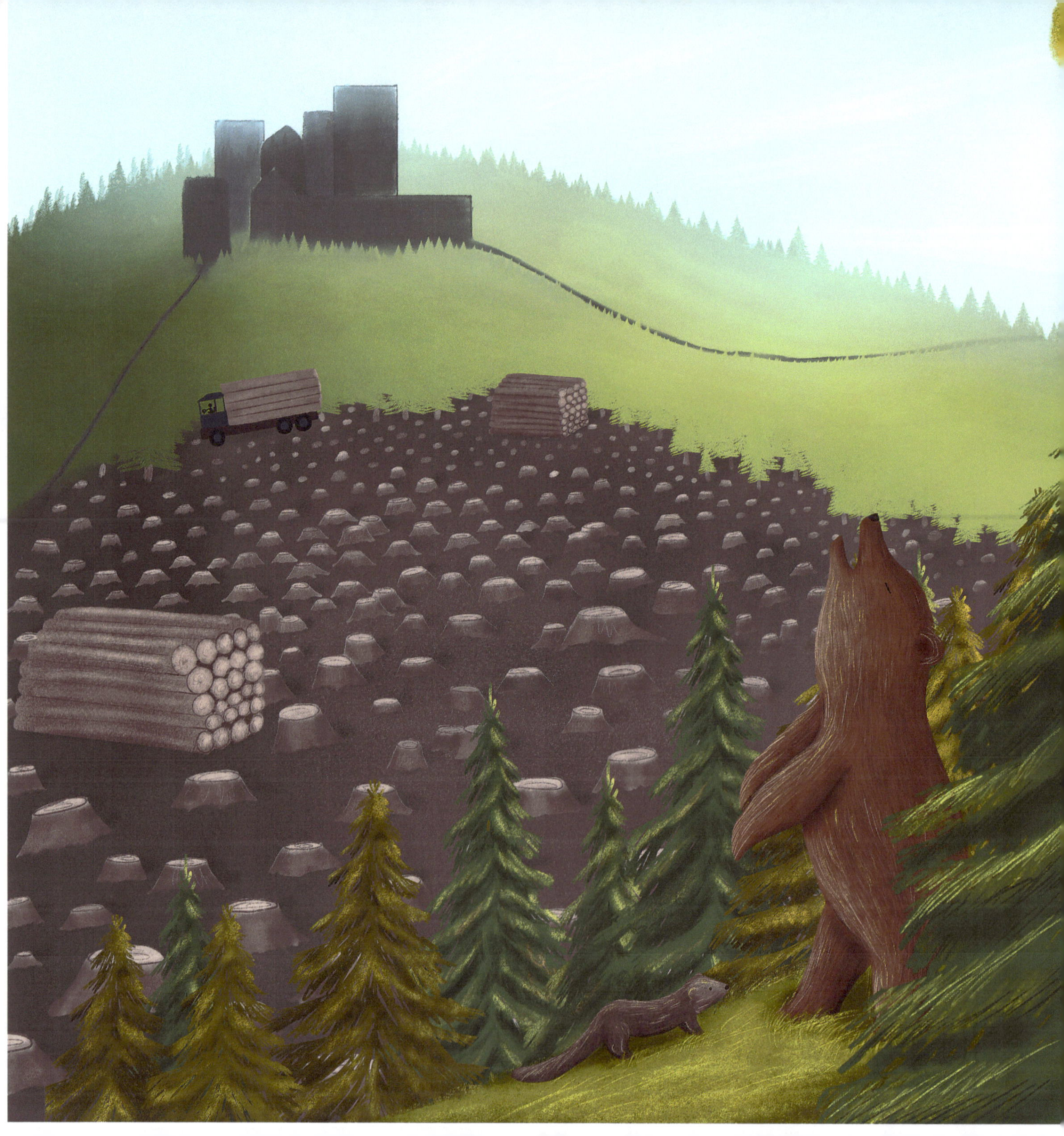

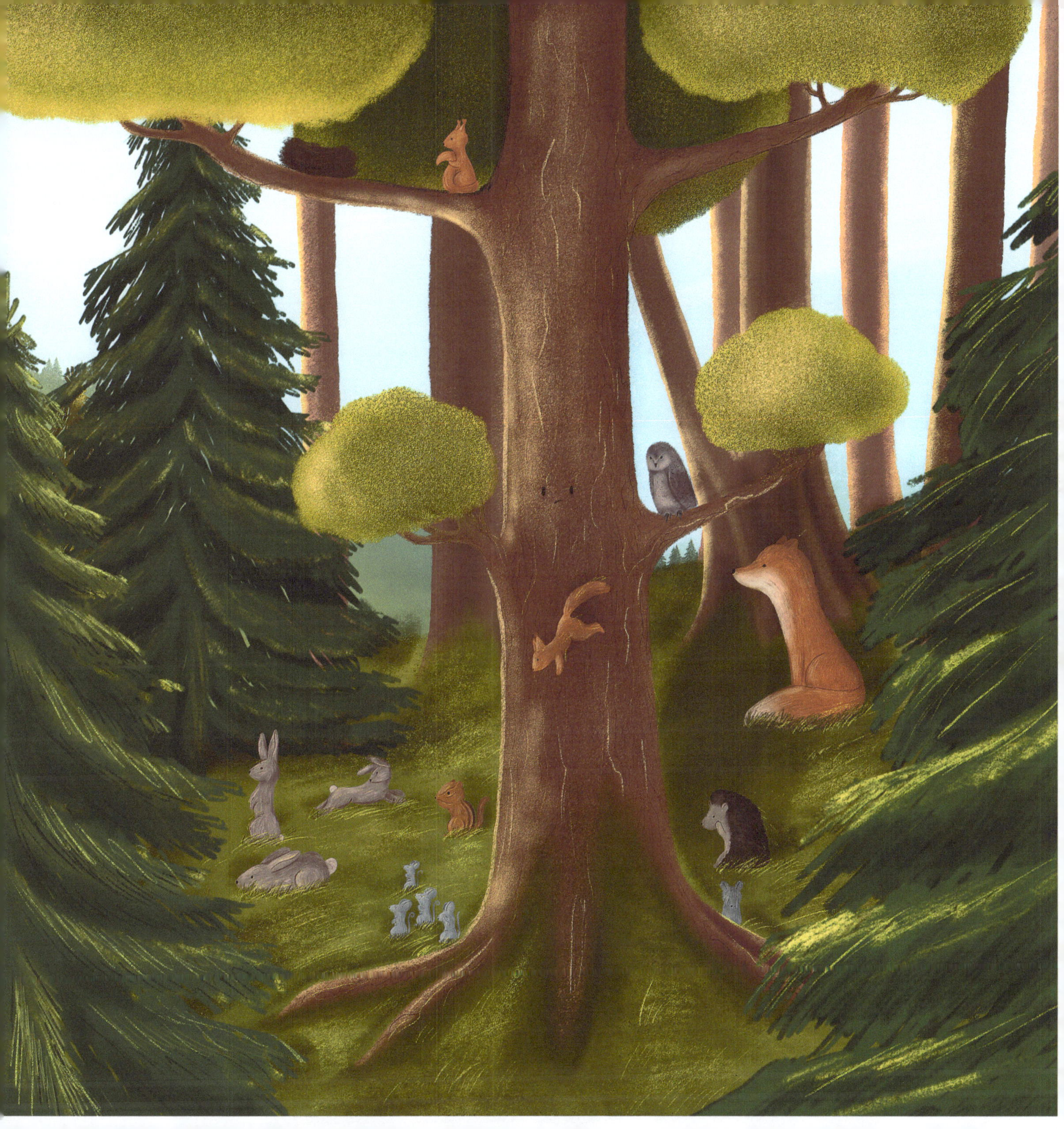

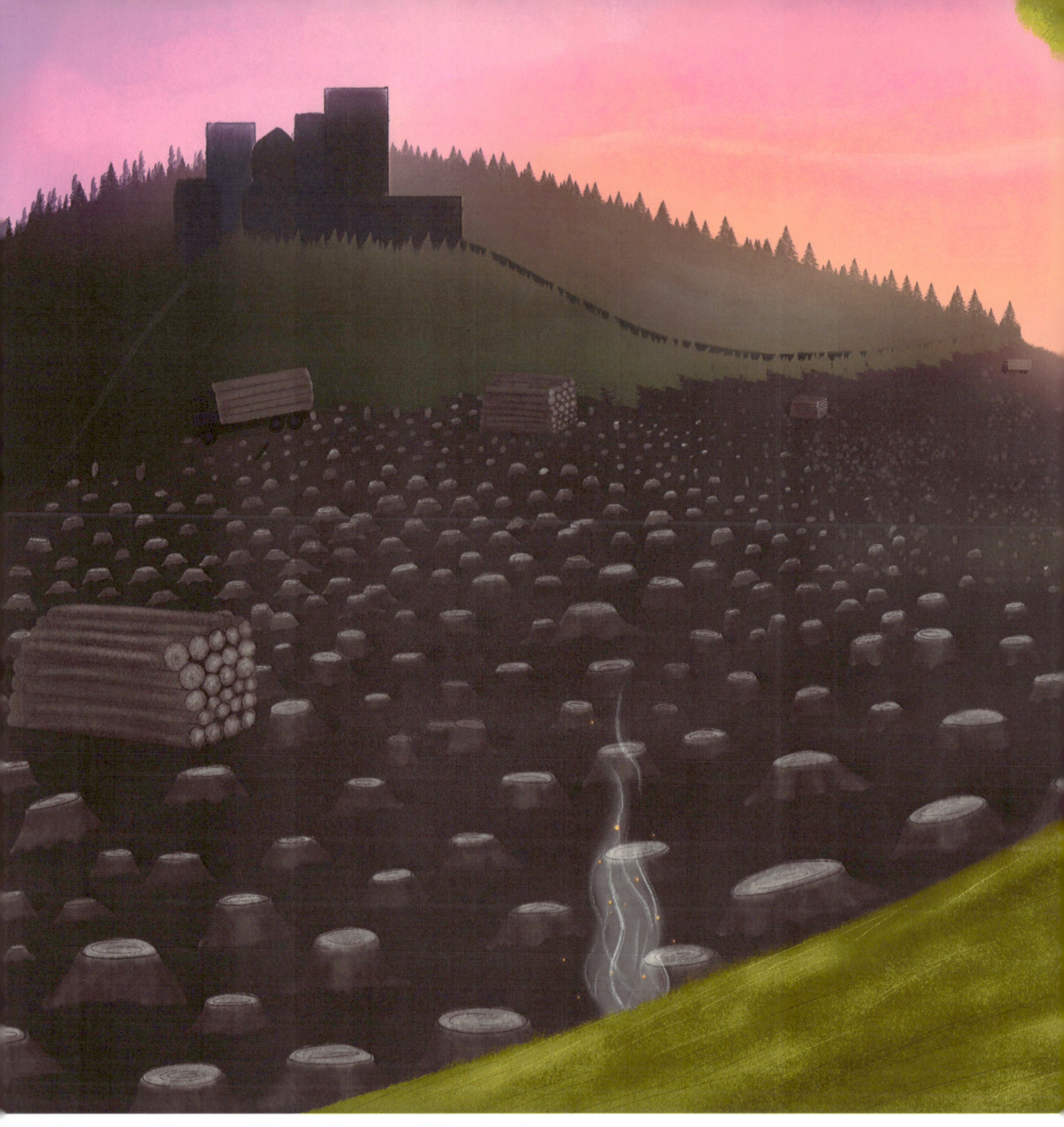

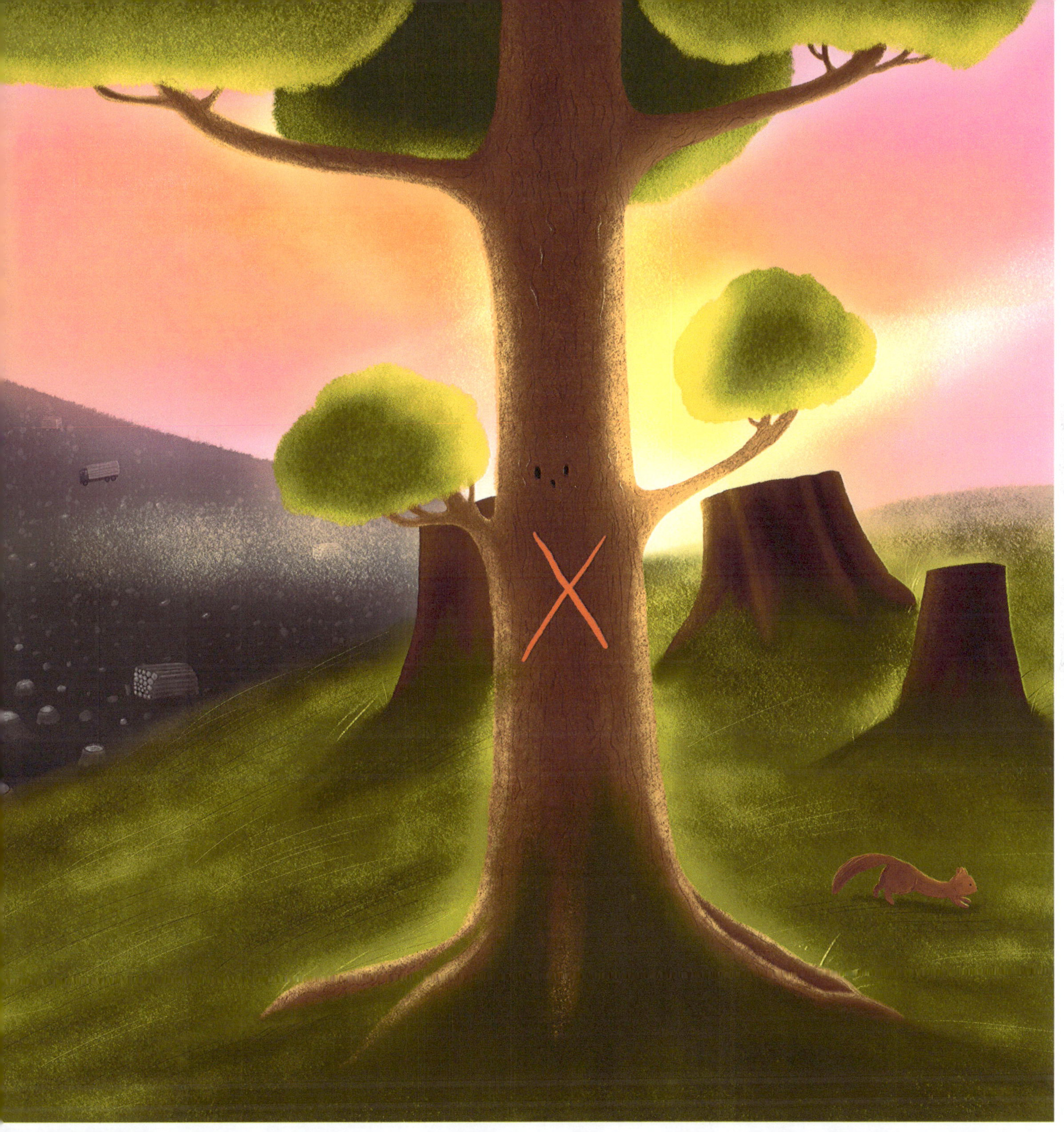

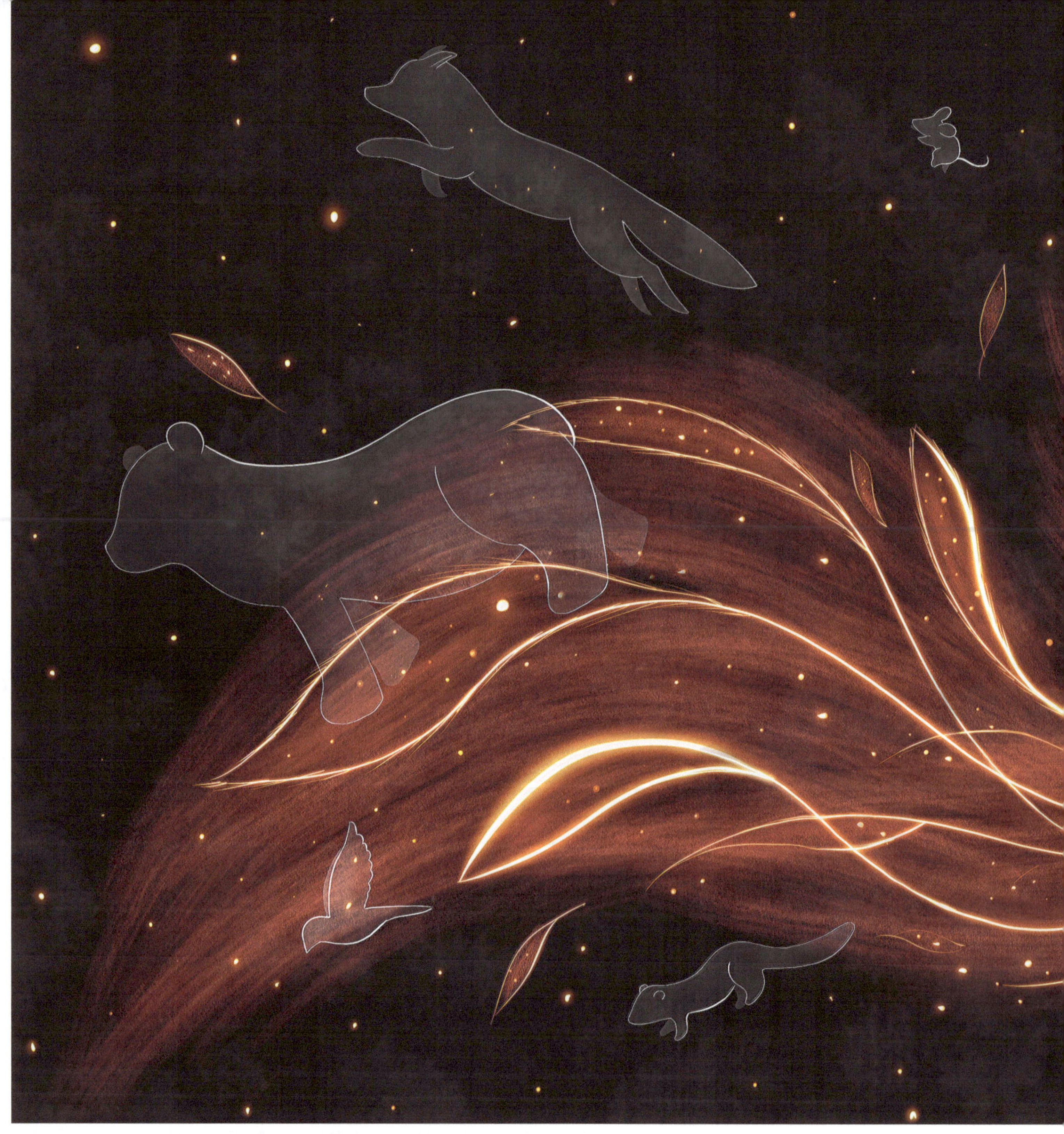

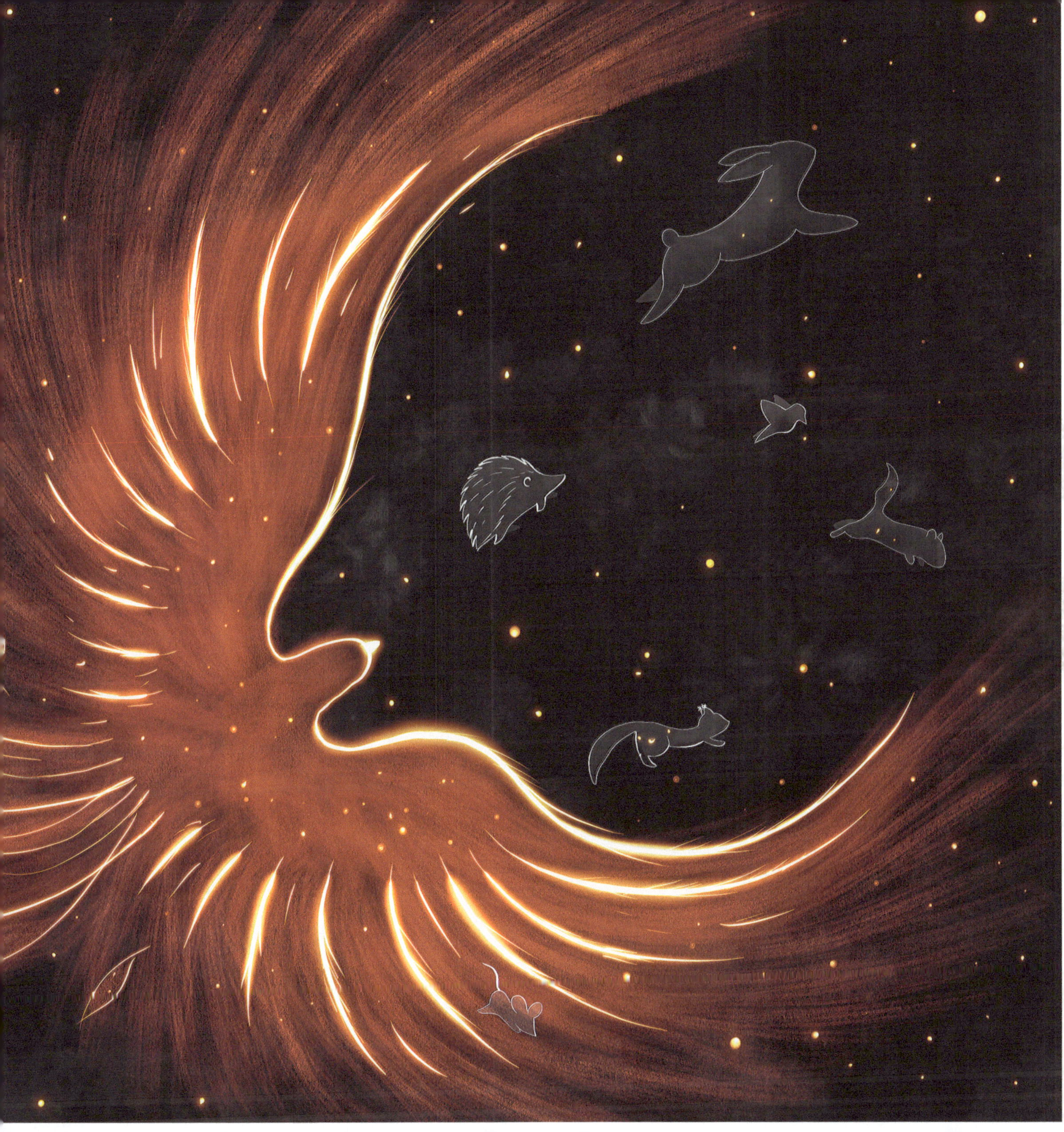

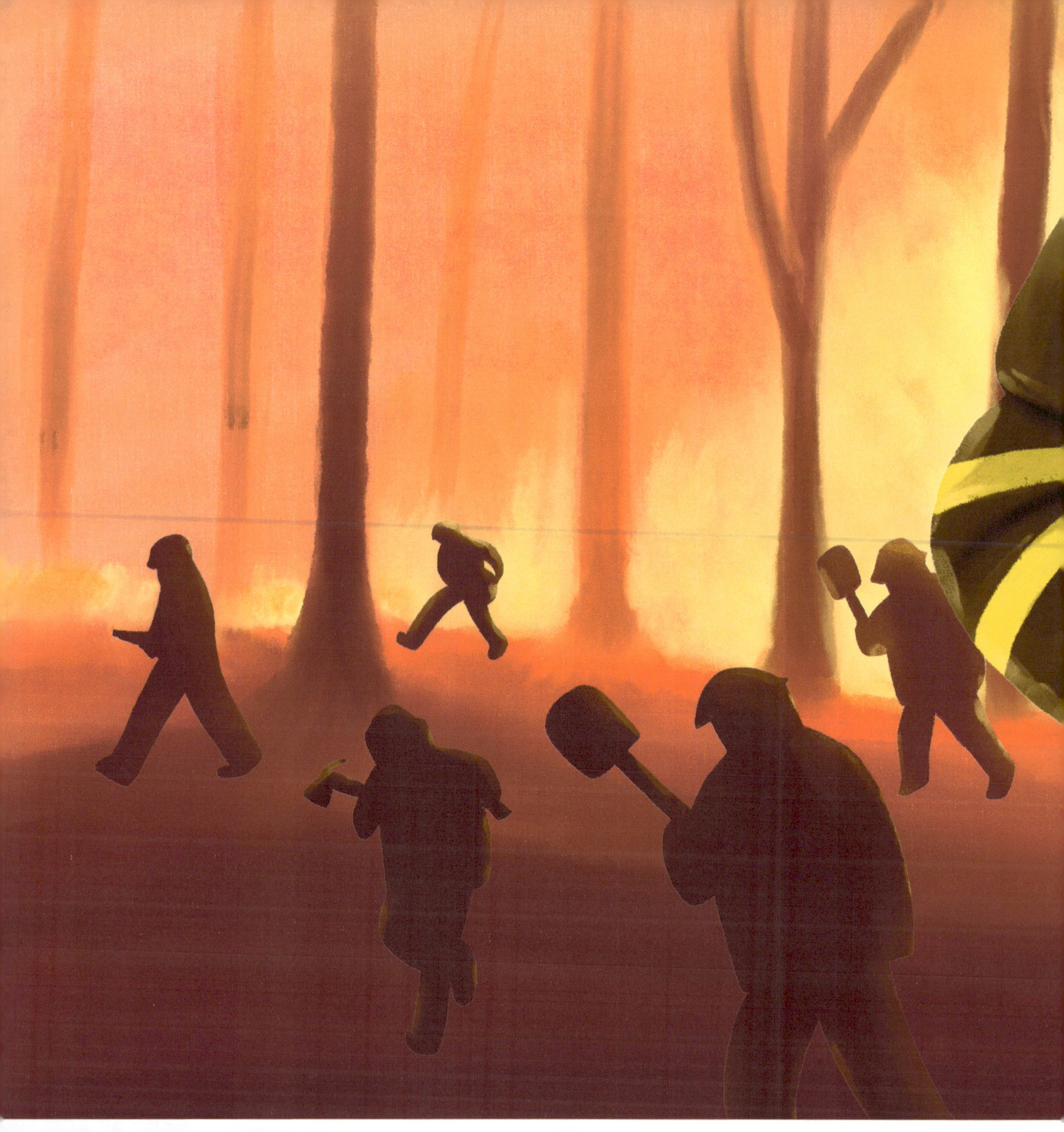

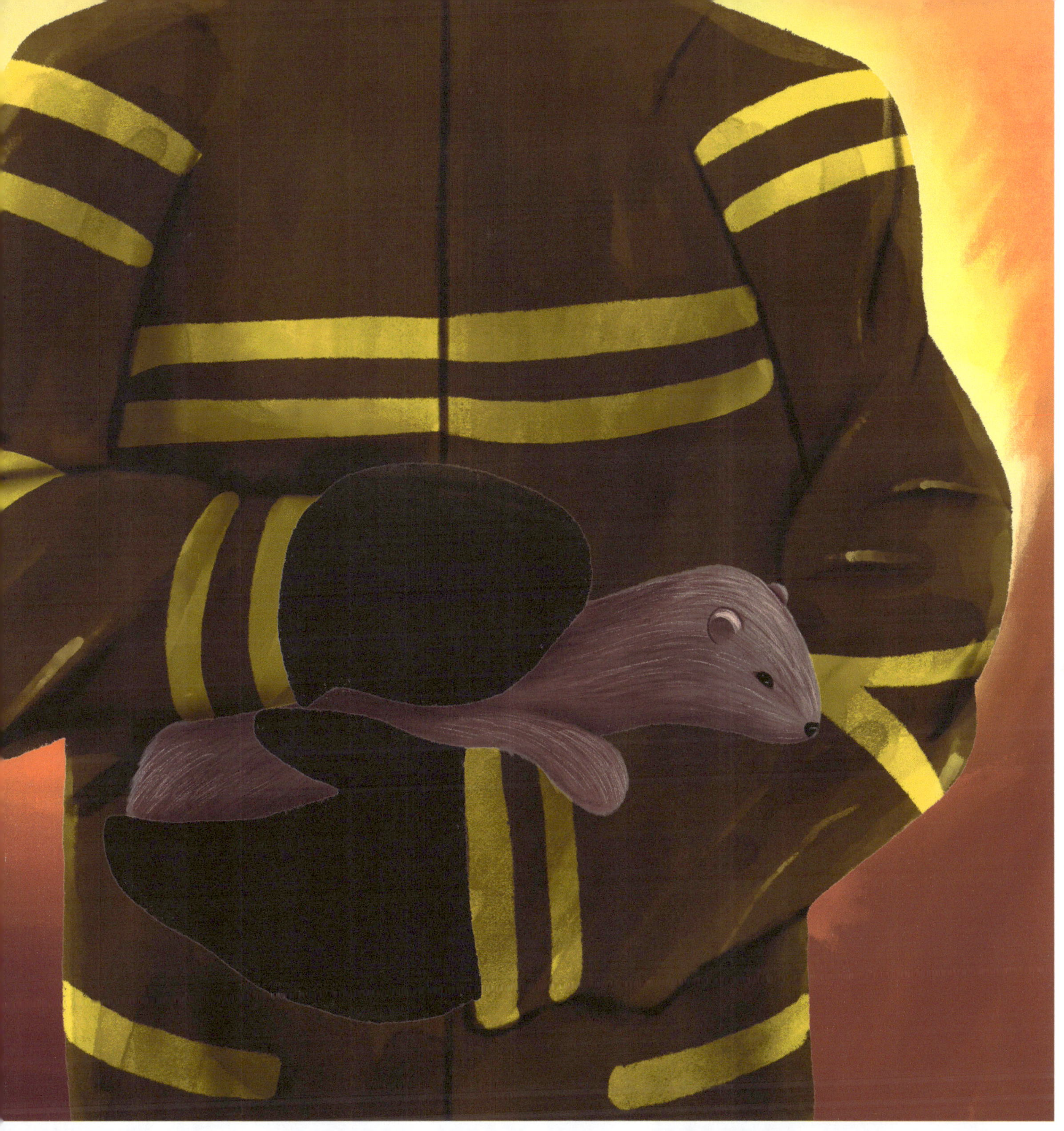

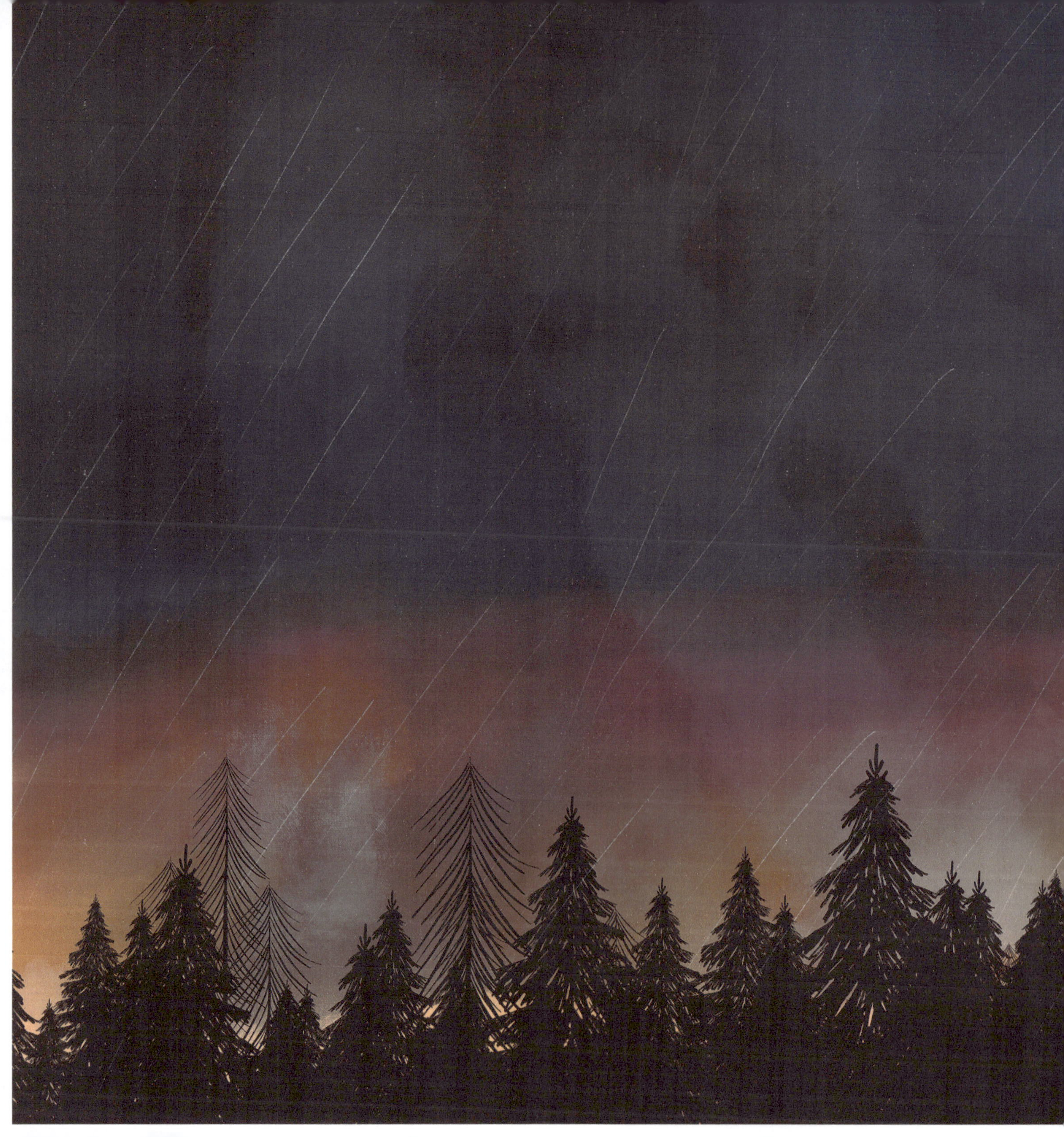

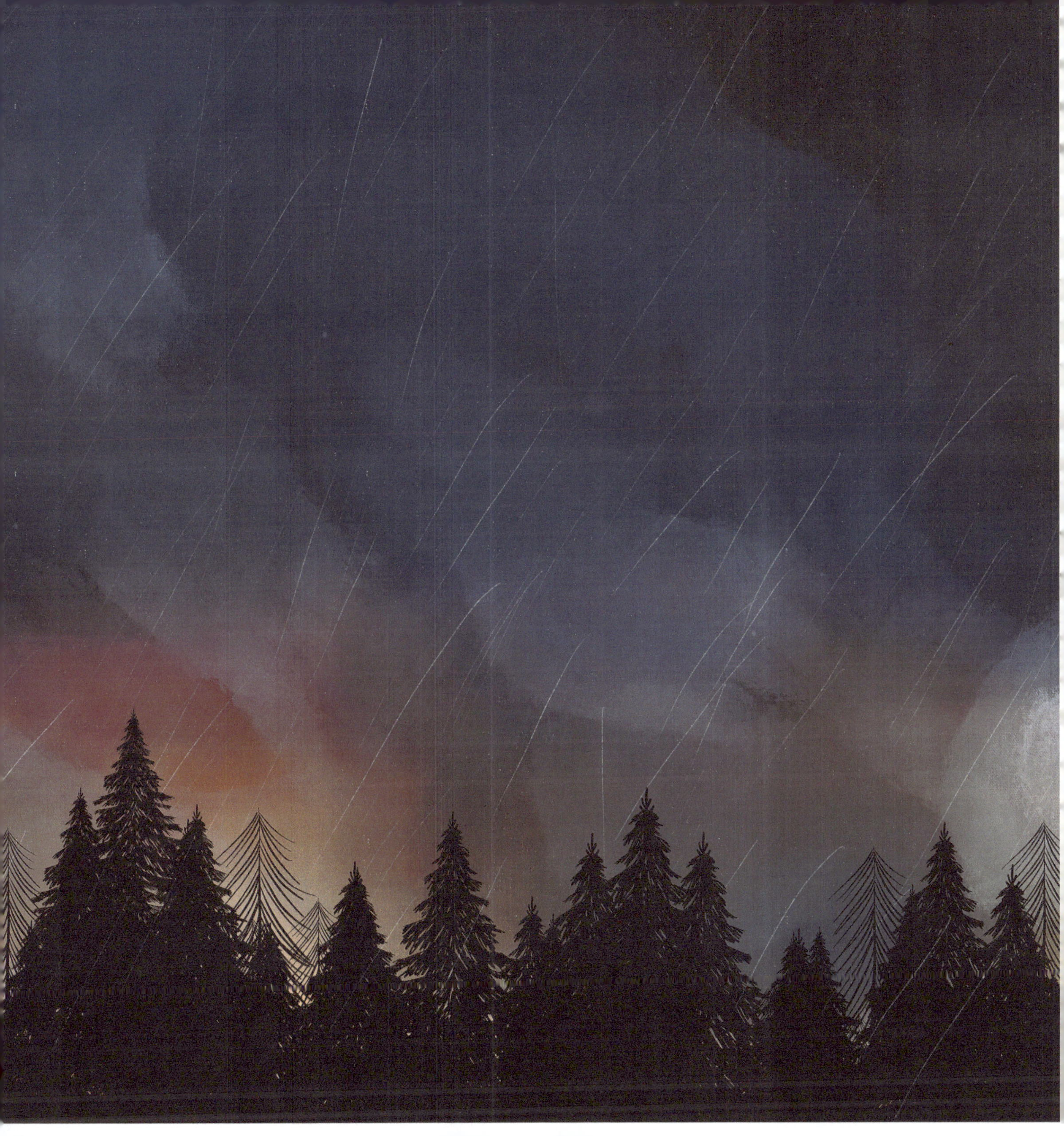

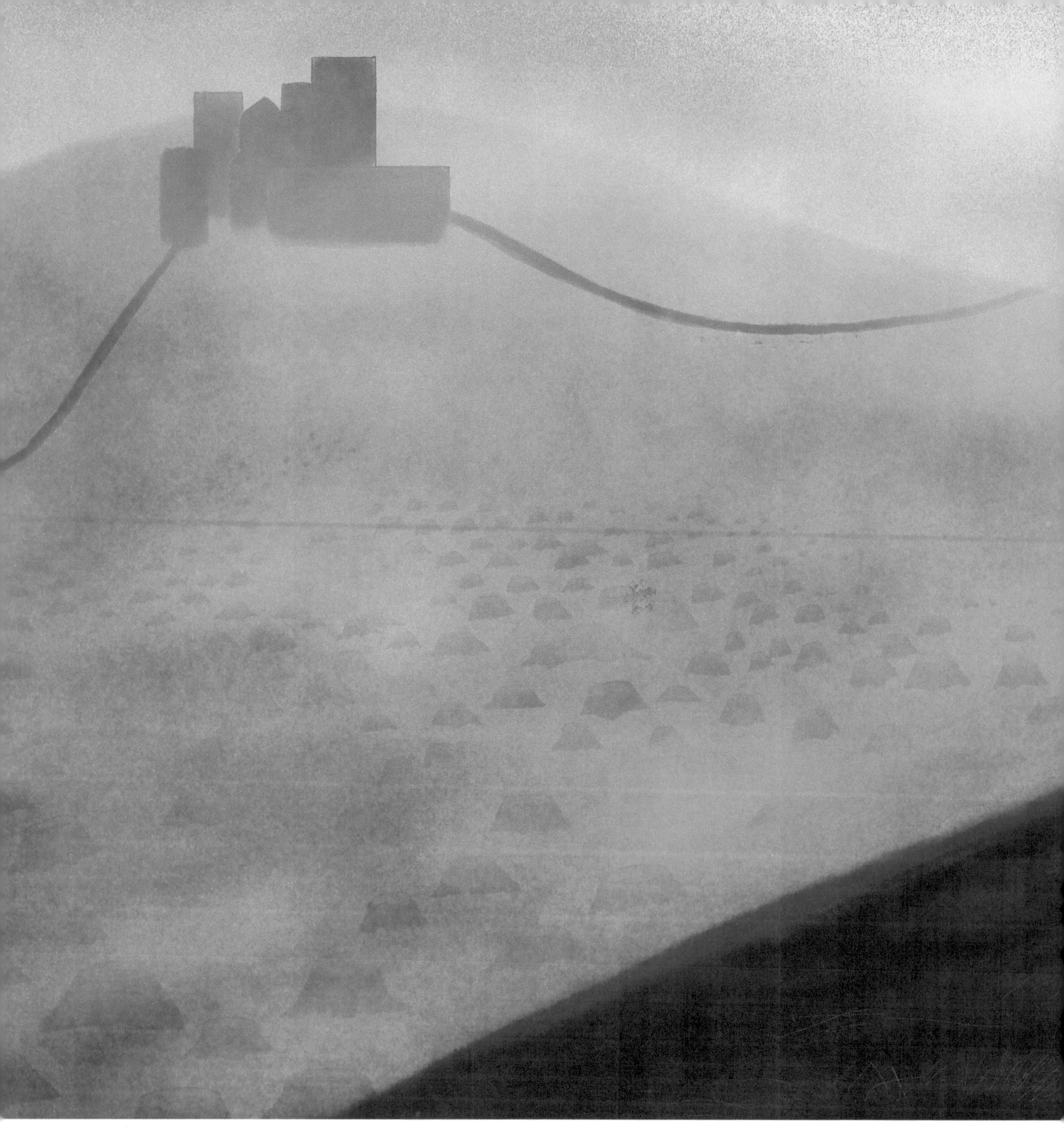

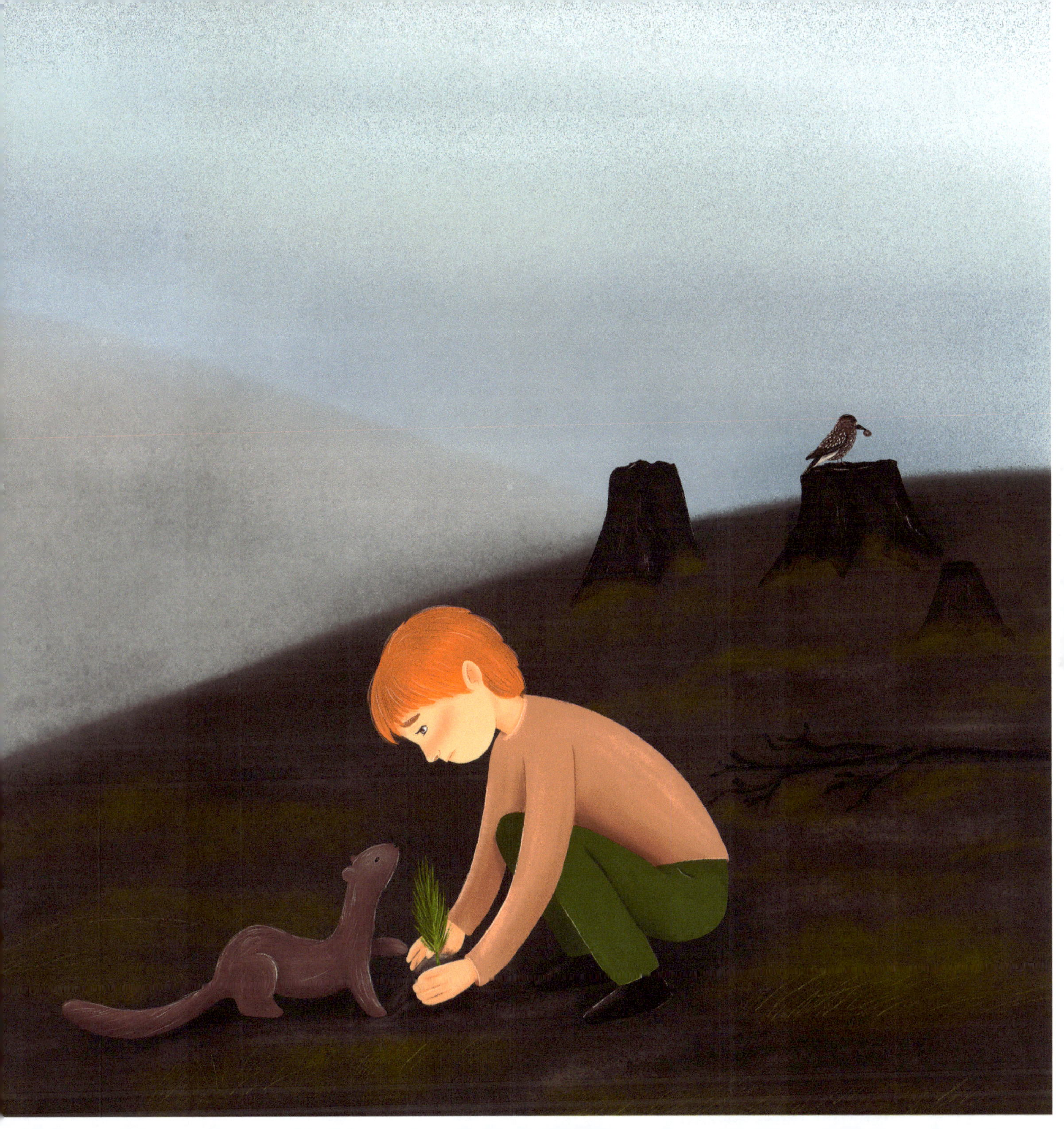

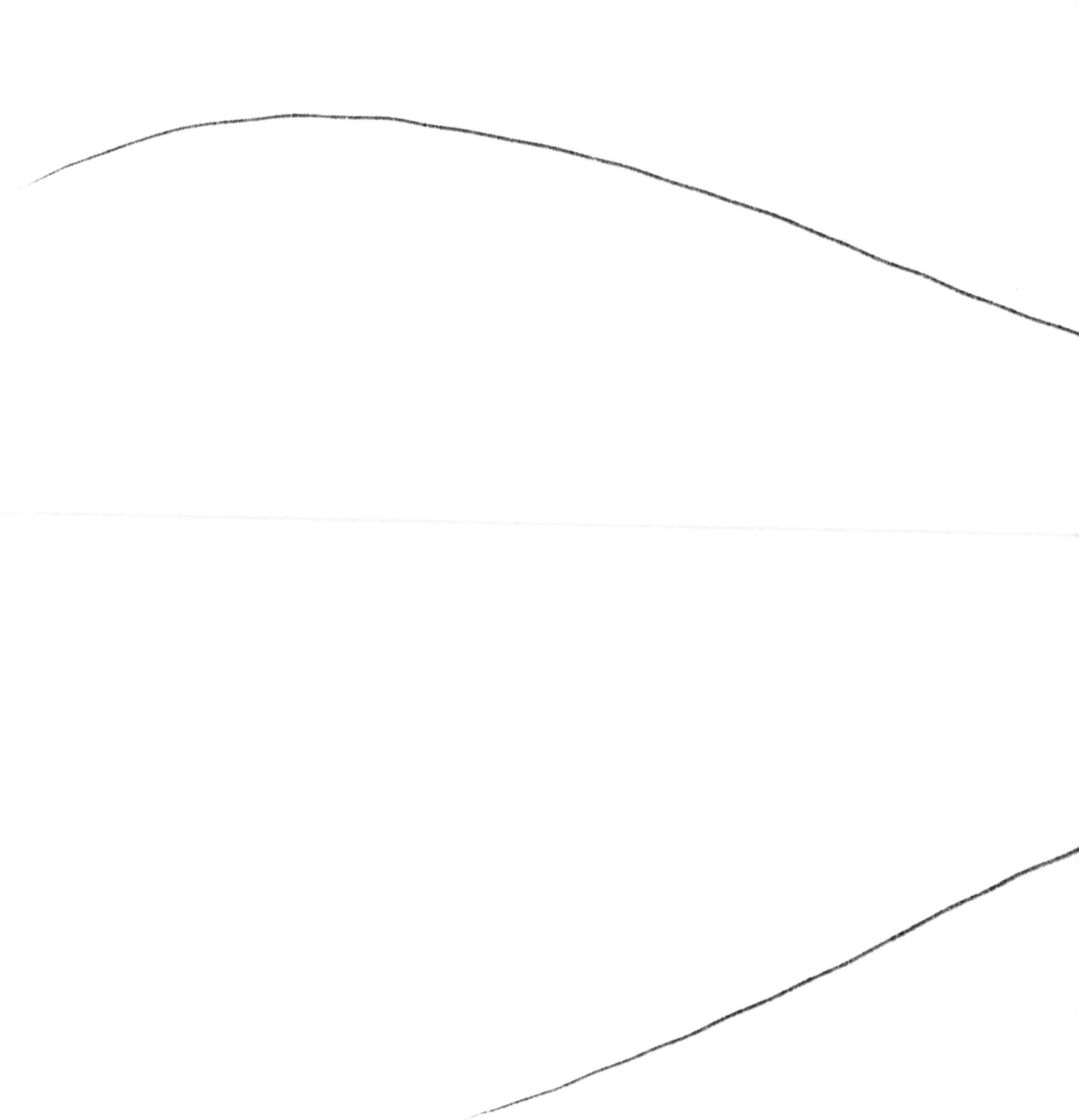

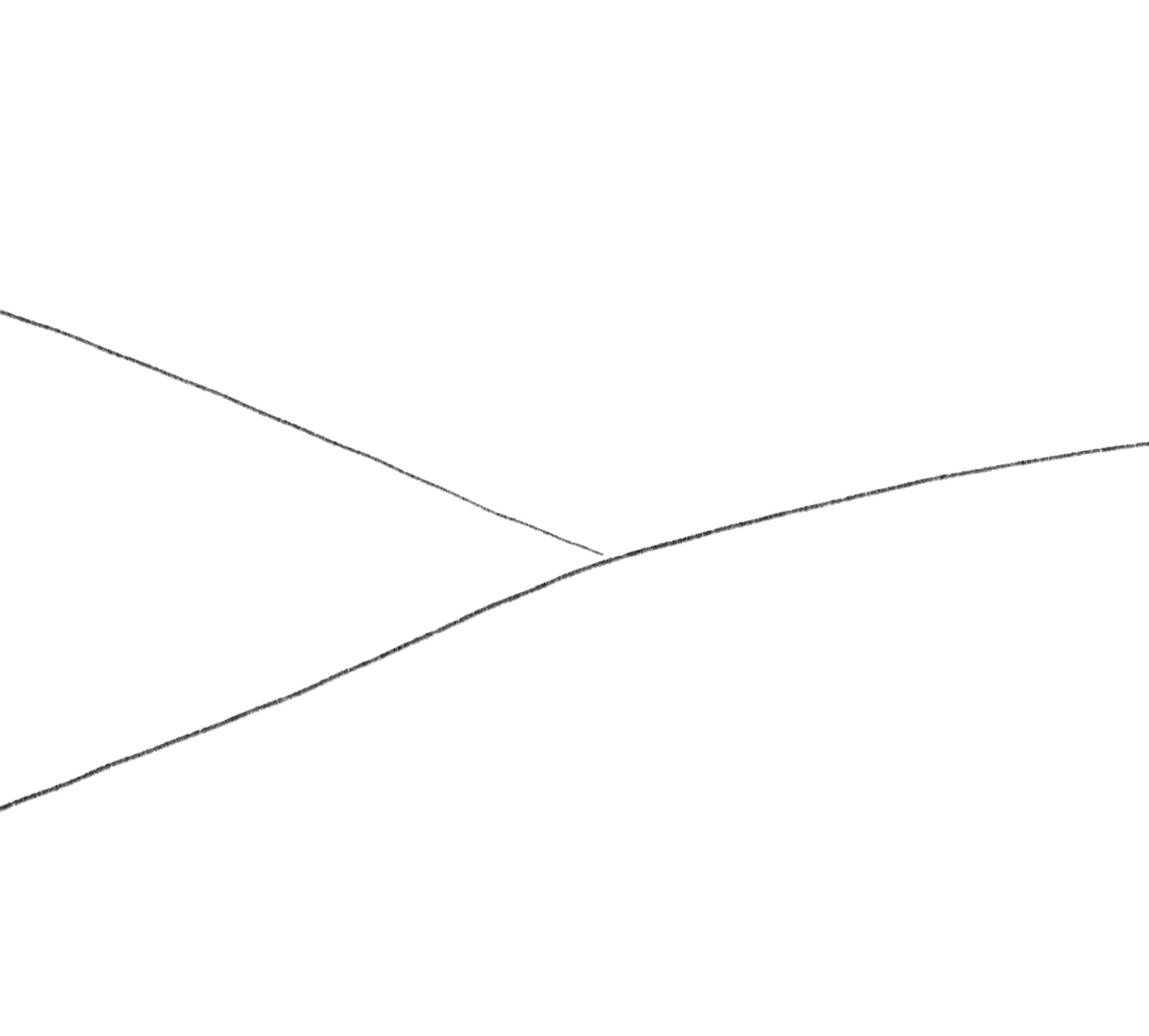